COME DINE WITH ME

COME DINE WITH ME

HOW TO THROW THE
PERFECT DINNER PARTY

641.568

Books

TRANSWORLD PUBLISHERS
61–63 Uxbridge Road, London W5 5SA
A Random House Group Company
www.rbooks.co.uk

First published in Great Britain in 2009 by Channel 4 Books
an imprint of Transworld Publishers

Text © David Sayer 2009
Recipes © Channel 4 2009

Photography: Dan Jones
Food stylist: SPK

The recipes in this book are based upon those submitted
by the enthusiastic amateur winners of the *Come Dine
With Me* television series.

Come Dine With Me is a Granada Production for
Channel 4 Television.

A CIP catalogue record for this book is available from
the British Library.

ISBN 9781905026623

Addresses for Random House Group Ltd companies outside
the UK can be found at: www.randomhouse.co.uk

The Random House Group Ltd Reg. No. 954009

The Random House Group Limited supports The Forest
Stewardship Council (FSC), the leading international forest-
certification organization. All our titles that are printed on
Greenpeace-approved FSC-certified paper carry the FSC
logo. Our paper procurement policy can be found at
www.rbooks.co.uk/environment

Designed by Smith & Gilmour, London
Typeset in Bliss
Printed & bound in Great Britain by Butler, Tanner & Dennis Ltd.

2 4 6 8 10 9 7 5 3 1

contents

about the programme

When it first appeared on Channel 4 in January 2005, no one could have dreamt just what a phenomenon *Come Dine With Me* would become. The first few weeks were a step in the dark for the channel, with those in charge of producing the show not quite knowing what the public would make of it. The format was simple, playing on the British love of dining – and looking inside each other's homes. Across the course of a week, five amateur chefs would take turns cooking dinner, in their own home, for the others – with the four guests marking the host. At the end of the five nights of – hopefully fine – dining, the top scorer walked off with a £1,000 prize.

Four years on and it's now a run-away success. The show has successfully transferred from daytime to prime-time on Channel 4, and featured a series of celebrity specials alongside the regular shows featuring ordinary people. The format sold to more than a dozen countries around the world, including the United States, France and Germany. It's even prompted lovers of the show to stage their own *Come Dine With Me* competitions – taking turns to cook and to mark each other's efforts.

Viewers enjoy watching the contestants try to outdo each other as hosts, poke around each other's houses – and generally try to outwit one another. But more than all of that,

Come Dine With Me is a cooking show, where enthusiastic home cooks parade their skills – and sometimes lack of them – in front of the nation. Most programmes feature original recipes that the cooks have dreamed up or developed for themselves.

Now this book brings together the best of those recipes: some have been used in their entirety, some have been edited or simplified for the everyday cook, all are based on the inspirational ideas of our prize-winning contestants. Alongside all that are lots of handy hints on how to plan the perfect dinner party, drawing on the experience of the hundreds of people who have taken part in the show.

A good dinner party is an amalgam of many things: fine food, washed down by the right wine, interspersed with sparkling conversation from guests who bond perfectly.

Easy to write down – but very difficult to get right. So over the next few pages, we'll try to bring you some advice on how to make your evening work – and warnings about where it can go wrong – when it comes to choosing your food, deciding who to put on the guest list, what to drink, and making sure that everyone enjoys each other's company around the table.

So whether you're a seasoned dinner party host, or a novice in the kitchen, this book should have something for you.

introduction

who to invite to dinner

Sounds like a silly question. Friends, of course, would seem to be the answer. Yes: but which of YOUR friends? Just because they're your friends, it doesn't mean they are friends with each other. So if you're a bit of a dinner party novice, already nervous about how your food is going to go down, then you don't need the added pressure of worrying about how your friends are getting on.

So make sure you bring the right group of people together around the table. It's almost as important as the food – as much for your sake as theirs. If you'd forgotten about a long-standing enmity between two groups of your mates, you'll have an evening that's more poisonous than an uncooked potato.

Even if they've never met, it's not necessarily guaranteed that they'll get on – you might delight in your rugby-loving mate Joe's risqué jokes, but it doesn't always follow that your opera-buff friend Ollie will enjoy a night in his company. So if you're not opting for mutual friends, then think long and hard about who you invite.

Of course, after a while, when you start to get into the swing of throwing dinner parties, you'll have wined and dined all your closest friends. So don't forget who you've invited and when, so you can work out what other combinations you can put together – remembering always to think about how compatible they'll be first.

You'll also start to come up with reasons for dinner parties: inviting the friends whose wedding you went to last summer; as long as you don't also invite the lecherous groomsman who made a pass at the bridesmaid sister of the bride.

Then there's the blind-date dinner party. An idea loved by all would-be matchmakers: they bring together two single friends over a delectable three-course meal, surrounded by other happy couples, who'll create such an atmosphere of love that they're bound to be dreaming of wedding venues before the night's out. Sounds like the scene from a Hollywood script? Well, no, actually it happens all the time up and down Britain: usually once, then hopefully never again. As it almost never works.

The already partnered guests are in on what's going on long before the two unsuspecting singletons arrive. But as soon as Lonely Heart Lady and Lonely Heart Man clap eyes on each other in a room otherwise populated only by happy couples, they'll instantly clock what's going on. And reach, embarrassed, for a drink. And another. And another. So by the time they sit down, they're beginning to slur more than slightly.

Then the seating plan goes disastrously wrong. Joe, married but nevertheless very flirtatious even though he's accompanied by his wife, ends up sat next to the evening's young, free and single woman. He cannot resist turning on the charm, and she's soon laughing at his jokes. Meanwhile, the male half of the host's would-be new super-couple is engaged in a long and protracted discussion about the state of the economy by Joe's wife who has a terribly interesting job (at least to her) in the Treasury. Then, whenever the host tries to turn the subject round to something the two spouse-less diners might share in common, Joe always seems to have a better story to tell, one that amuses Lonely Heart Lady. When Lonely Heart Man tries to chip in, his jokes are met with a deafening silence.

Overcome by mortification, he attacks the wine even harder. So his next joke is met by an even longer silence, and so it goes on, until he manages to spill a bottle of plonk over Lonely Heart Lady. Clumsy over-exaggerated mopping up follows, leading to lots of embarrassment all round. Meanwhile, everyone apart from Joe is squirming in their seats at the discomfort of it all – or enjoying every minute, if they're of a more sadistic nature.

By the time the night's over, Joe's wife is in a huff because Joe's lavishing more attention on Lonely Heart Lady; Lonely Heart Lady is desperate for the number of her new-found friend, while Lonely Heart Man is so drunk he can barely get his shoes on. When he wakes up the following morning, he'll have a sore head and be cursing his friend, the host, for making a fool of him with the cack-handed attempt at matchmaking. And he'll be vowing never to set foot in the host's house ever again until he has found himself a girlfriend, for fear that the whole ghastly business will repeat itself.

Meanwhile, you, the host, are cursing yourself for being so stupid. But a month later, the over-optimistic matchmaker side of your brain takes over, and you decide to try the same daft thing all over again. Don't. After all, when have you ever heard of anyone starting a wedding speech with the words: 'When we met during a shameless piece of matchmaking over dinner at John's, it was love at first sight.'

Remember, introductions are often organized at parties, so people can mingle with others, and then beat a hasty retreat if they quickly realize they have nothing in common. Or in bars, so that one person can walk in, take a look at the other and walk straight out again to avoid any embarrassment. Or escape through the back door of the bar midway through the date.

But at a dinner party there's no way out. Wedging people together at a dinner table who've never met before, knowing they can't escape for at least two hours (unless they have a terrible excuse up their sleeve), and expecting them to enjoy themselves, with everyone else looking on wondering if they'll hit it off, is a recipe for disaster.

There is another dreaded dinner-party scenario that most of us will have to go through at one stage or another in our lives: catering for our parents and those of our partner. Inevitably it will be the first time they've ever met. One set won't like dining out, while another set lives just too far away to justify meeting up for a quick cup of tea. So they'll both come up with the same idea: 'Why don't we have dinner [or more usually lunch] at your place, dear?'

The contestants on *Come Dine With Me* are given £125 to pay for ingredients for their three-course meal, along with wine.

No matter how long you try to put it off, you'll have to succumb one day, when your stock of excuses runs dry. Then, stretching in front of you is the afternoon, or evening, that fills you with utter fear. Your parents – who always drink too much and say the wrong things, whether it's lunch or dinner – will meet your future in-laws who think a small sherry followed by a glass of low-alcohol lager is the road to ruin.

If you are a woman, you have to cope with the ordeal of catering for your future mother-in-law, who will be watching everything like a hawk to find out whether you can keep her son in the culinary style to which he has become accustomed.

If you're a man, you'll be scrutinized minutely by your partner's mother who suspects her daughter's hitched up with a layabout who doesn't know a spatula from a soufflé, drinks too much and is generally a liability about the house for everything other than fixing up one of those XY-box thingies to the telly, and pummelling away at it for hours on end.

So come up with a plan of attack. Know exactly what your parents like and dislike to eat and cater accordingly. You might hate soggy, overdone vegetables, steak and kidney pie and sponge pudding, but if they love it, then cook it. Then make a list of all the jobs you're going to do, and divide them equally between each of you: one to do the starter, the other to do the dessert, while you both help out preparing the main.

Try out all the dishes at least once well in advance. Even borrow an older neighbour to test out whether your custard is the right thickness or your broccoli is overcooked enough: remember there is a reason that old people eat their greens: because they've boiled all the nasty taste out of it.

Practise saying, politely, but firmly, 'No, Mother/Mrs Smith, it's fine, we don't need any help, we'll be with you in a minute,' at least twenty-five times before the big day. Start again if there's any hint of anger, weariness or impatience creeping into your voice, until you can say it twenty-five times with perfect equanimity on each occasion. Because if you don't have to say it twenty-five times when everyone's round, you'll have to say it twenty-four or twenty-six.

Don't talk to your parents on the phone for at least two weeks before the date of the meal: that way you'll have plenty of conversational gambits up your sleeve. Secretly find out from your brother or sister what they've been up to, so you can uncover suitably innocent topics to talk about. Then compare notes to work out what they might be interested in talking about together.

When the day dawns, do as much as you possibly can in advance – because the longer you leave your parents alone together, the sooner they will start on the embarrassing stories about your childhood that you'd really rather your partner didn't know – or at least only found out when he or she had that wedding ring on their finger.

If you're really unlucky, they'll have arrived with visual props: photo albums of you buck naked as a six-month-old baby, complete with rolls of fat that a Sumo wrestler would be proud of. That's where that list of conversational topics comes in brilliantly handy to divert attention. And your skilfully prepared food can be deployed slightly earlier than usual.

When it comes to serving the food, take turns: one in the kitchen, the other at the table, apart, perhaps, from the more complicated main course. That way, you look like a team – even if one of you is actually a hopeless cook and has done nothing for the preparation, you can at least make it appear as though you know what you're doing by plating up the starter or the pudding, along with stirring the gravy (the chances are there will be gravy: this is your parents we're talking about) and dishing up the (very well-cooked) veg.

Keep a steady supply of wine for everyone – bar the pair of you. There'll always be one of the mums or dads who's not drinking, so if you start slurring, you might not notice, but they certainly will.

Finally, there's the problem of how to end the lunch or dinner. If it's dinner, then they'll have to get home at some point. But if it's lunch, it could go on for a long time. Indeed, so long that one of the fathers soon utters the dreaded words: 'I'm feeling a bit peckish again – could you rustle us up something?' Even though you've just served them a meal that's stuffed with enough calories to see Paula Radcliffe through two marathons.

So come up with an excuse for something you have to do at a particular time as a way of bringing proceedings to a close – not too early, as that looks rude, but not too late as they'll stay until the last minute. Make it out of the house and preferably something they cannot involve themselves in: tickets for a play in a tiny theatre that sold out long ago; a birthday party for friends. And that will eventually bring the whole afternoon to an end. Hopefully your parents will leave as friends – but not so much so that they're already pencilling a date in the diary for a replay in a month's time because your flat is so handily placed between them. Of course, if they don't get on, you only have to endure it for the afternoon, and you never have to go through it again!

how to plan a menu

Once you've decided who to invite, you can then think about the other essential ingredient for any dinner party: the food. Planning a menu is a thing that takes time. So give yourself plenty of it. And by that we don't mean leafing through all the cookbooks you can lay your hands on the night before. If you get the food right, the rest of the evening should follow. If you get it wrong, then you'll have a memorable meal on your hands – but for all the wrong reasons.

So here are a few simple tips.

Think of recipes that complement each other. There's no point in cooking your favourite dishes if they don't go together as you'll only leave your guests bemused at best, and dyspeptic at worst. Frog's legs followed by rogan josh, all topped off with treacle sponge and custard, is probably only of interest to a half-French, half-Indian who developed a taste for heavy puds at boarding school: and how many people who fit that bill are you going to have round for dinner? You may laugh, but stranger menus have appeared on *Come Dine With Me*.

Think about the time of year and the occasion. (And don't overreach yourself.) If it's summer, a substantial roast joint probably isn't ideal. While a cold starter, tepid main and light fruit pudding will hardly have your diners ready for braving a bitterly cold winter's night. Not only that, but you might not find the ingredients for the light fruit pudding (unless, of course, you don't mind them being flown in from halfway round the world).

Catering for a family gathering at Christmas is completely different from cooking an informal supper for friends. Don't be too showy: trying to cook food that you tasted at that wonderful Michelin-starred restaurant will stick in your friends' throats – especially if they're not great cooks. They might love the food, but they'll hate you for showing off, and will be too scared to invite you round to theirs. So you'll become the one that does all the entertaining but never receives the invites back.

And, of course, there is also the possibility that if you overreach yourself, the food will taste disgusting; and you will not only never be invited round to theirs again because they've never forgiven you for cooking such terrible food, but you will never see them at your place either, because they don't want to be put through such awful suffering ever again.

Opt for a menu that you can prepare ahead as much as possible. You're hosting a dinner party, so your guests shouldn't leave wondering what you look like because you've been stuck in the kitchen all night. Choose dishes you like, but don't opt for all three courses that you have to prepare from scratch after your guests have arrived. Otherwise, while you're agitated over the Aga, they're becoming slowly sloshed on the sofa, as they work their way through the wine to hide their nerves because their host isn't there. And that means by the time the main course is served, you'll have a load of drunks on your hands, who won't appreciate the food – or your sober serious conversation.

Unless your name's Gordon Ramsay, don't decide to do something you've never cooked before. Even if your name is Gordon Ramsay, it's still probably wise advice. It will take twice as long, because you take extra care over the recipe, so distracting you from hosting duties. And all that extra care won't guarantee it will turn out right: a) because you don't know what it's supposed to look like – it certainly won't look like the picture in the cookbook, because nothing anyone ever cooks does; and b) because all ovens are different, it will either be over-cooked or under-cooked. Of course, there's

a chance that it will come out right. But it's about as likely as you becoming Prime Minister. So don't take the risk. If you absolutely must do a recipe you've never done before, then at least try it out first. That way there's some chance you'll get it right when it matters – although you'll have to inflict a dodgy trial run on your nearest and dearest, who thus might not be talking to you when it comes round to the dinner party. If the trial run is a disaster, someone is trying to tell you something. Take the hint, ditch the recipe and choose something else.

Know your guests. You might love foie gras, but if your best mate's new girlfriend is secretary of the local vegetarian society, and you only discover this as you're serving the starter, then you're in trouble. And don't expect your friend to keep you in the know – especially if your friend's a guy. They'll assume they've told you already, when they haven't. Then when they see the offending pâté, they'll say: 'I did tell you Susan was a vegetarian, didn't I?'

You could, of course, say, 'No, you didn't.' But making your friend look stupid in front of his new partner by saying that the only thing he's told you about Susan is that she has nice legs, is rude. And will guarantee a frosty atmosphere for the rest of the evening. Instead, to avoid these kinds of uncomfortable scenario, ask your guests what they don't like long before they get anywhere near your front door. No one will be offended, and that way you'll know everyone will eat the food. Without having to attend A and E because you've brought on their nut allergy.

When choosing a recipe, think about the equipment you need to make it. If the recipe says 'blend', that means you need a blender or food processor, not just a wooden spoon and some good arm muscles. And if you haven't got one, you're in trouble. So when selecting a dish, don't read through the cooking instructions for the first time while your guests are seated next door in the dining room, because it will call for that vital piece of kit you haven't got, and your guests will be going hungry – or badly fed. Instead, read right through to the end of the recipe well in advance so you can check you have every last thing you need to make the food. If you don't, you have just two options, and one of them is not 'I'll busk it on the night', as that most certainly isn't how Raymond Blanc won his Michelin stars. Instead, go out and buy the offending item; or, if you don't want to run up a debt catering for a few ungrateful friends, then ditch the recipe and choose something else that doesn't require a couple of hundred quid's worth of cooking kit.

Make sure you feed your guests enough … Salad, followed by a piece of fish with salad and, er, fruit salad for pudding, will see them stopping off for a kebab on the way home. And turning down your next invitation to dinner.

… but don't feed them so much they start to look like Mr Blobby. They'll feel uncomfortable, and will only spend hours stuck on your sofa, because they're too bloated to get up, when you're desperate to do the washing up, put out the rubbish and hit the sack.

Once you've put together a draft menu, work out the timings. Calculate how long it's going to take to prepare everything; then add at least 50 per cent extra time: if the recipe book says 10 minutes, then allow 15 for luck. Next, note down how long everything's going to take to cook. Step three: work out when you want to serve your various dishes (preferably the starter before the main course, and the side dish of spuds to go with the main rather than the dessert).

From there, work backwards to find out at what time you have to put your dishes on to cook (not forgetting to add an extra 10 minutes for preheating the oven). The time for putting on the dishes is the latest time you can finish the preparation: so start working backwards again to discover when you need to start prep.

If possible, also add in time for meeting and greeting your guests, so that there will be a pause in your preparation. Then double the amount of time you need to allow, because transport being what it is in this country, there's a good chance that someone will be late, then you'll be leaving your guests to get to know each other, while you're dashing into the kitchen to cook. Factor in time not only for arrivals and fixing drinks, but also a decent amount of time to spend with your guests to make sure the conversation's flowing before you have to return to your cooking duties.

The process of planning should also reveal whether you have to cook two things at once: e.g. a sauce and some fish. Yep, the dreaded multi-tasking. The trickiest part of a dinner party. When everything can so easily fall apart. Especially if you're a guy. If battling away at two different recipes at the same time fills you with dread, then there's only one thing for it. Change your menu.

By the time you've done all that you will have a timetable, which hopefully will resemble a comprehensible plan of attack. The schedule should tell you what time you have to start doing everything. If it means starting at four, but you'll only get in from work at five, you'll have to think again, as

your diners won't thank you if they have to wait for hours for their food.

Keep a record of what you've cooked for whom. If you love throwing dinner parties, but only have a small repertoire, then there's nothing worse than your friends turning up for the third pot roast in three months – especially if, each time, it doesn't taste as good as the previous one. If you are serious about throwing dinner parties – and of course you are! – think about keeping a dinner party book, and note who you invited, when, what you fed them and what you drank, and how much of a success it was.

buying your ingredients

You've chosen your menu, and you're dying to impress your guests with your culinary expertise. But before you get down to the tricky business of cooking, you need to buy your ingredients. Simple, of course. Well, no, it's not. Who hasn't got midway through cooking a recipe only to find out they're missing a vital ingredient? Or haven't bought enough of another one? Go on, admit it: you've done it.

We've all done it. That's because we're a nation that loves shopping for everything. Except for food. Because supermarkets are horrible places, and most of us aren't lucky enough to live somewhere with a butcher, baker and greengrocer all handily situated one next to the other. So we shop badly for our groceries and forget a few things. And that can scupper even the best-planned dinner party.

So here are a few iron rules to remember when you go shopping.

Make a list. Easy. Don't need to worry too much about that. Until you start cooking. And half your ingredients are missing. By which time it's far too late to go back. Go through the recipes and make a list of absolutely everything you need. Then get someone to read out the ingredients suggested in the recipe while you cross-check with your shopping list.

Write down how much of everything you need. Just noting down 'carrots' is no good.

When you come home with two, and the recipe says two kilos, you're in trouble.

Calculate the amount you need for the number of people you're inviting – and their appetites. Most recipes will say how many they serve. So work out whether you need to increase what you're buying if you're inviting more. Or if you're inviting hulking rugby mates who eat twice as much as everyone else. Or just plain greedy people.

Never assume you have something. If you do, there's a good chance your partner will have used it up on that cheeky little soiree he had with his mates while you were away on work. Then on the big night, when you come to cook, you'll spend ages looking in your cupboards for it, muttering, 'I know it's in here,' or 'Where has he put it?' All to no avail. So always check that the ingredient you assume you have in stock is in the cupboard. And also look to see whether it has a sell-by date older than that on Peter Andre's pop career.

Don't just check the ingredients in the recipes. Think about the other things that people can consume. Nibbles. Salt and pepper for the salt and pepper cellars. Limes or lemons for the gin and tonics. Tonic for the gin and tonic …

Order in advance: or have an alternative to cook. That fancy recipe with capers, wild mushrooms and Belgian endive is all very good, but when the staff at your local store don't even know what you're talking about when you ask whether it's in stock, still less have it on the shelves, then you're up against it even before you've started cooking. Unless you have ordered in advance. Or you have an alternative dish you can buy ingredients for instead.

Take the list with you. Equally obvious. But who hasn't got to the supermarket only to discover they have left their list behind? Then, there are only two options: guessing or going home. Naturally everyone opts for guessing. But they should have plumped for going home, as when you get back to read the list on your kitchen table, there will be something missing – and that one thing will be vital to the recipe, so you will have to go back to the shops.

Buy more than you need. If you're worried about any of the dishes you're making, then make sure you buy – or have in stock – at least twice as much as you need. Because then if the first one turns out to be a disaster, you don't have to rush out to the shops at the last minute to the buy replacement ingredients. Never forget the iron law of dinner-party prep: if you have too much, it won't go wrong, but if you don't have enough, then you're sure to need more.

Obviously, if you think you're a completely hopeless cook, then buy three or four times as much as you need so that you can have three or four goes. Although I'd say that if you are onto the fourth attempt, you're not really destined to get it right, so reach for the ice cream instead.

Buy some kitchen roll. Much the best thing for wiping up spillages just before serving the food: unless you want your guests to enjoy the odour of stale kitchen cloth to accompany their dinner.

Buy some plasters. Preferably those blue ones, that you can spot when you carve into the pudding. If you have a supply, you won't cut your finger; but if you don't have any, you can bet you will.

choosing the drink

No dinner party is complete without drink – and choosing it is almost as important as compiling the menu. You might serve up a delicious dish but wash it down with paint-stripping plonk, and that's what your guests will remember when they get home.

So spend a bit of time sorting out your wine. If you don't have a clue about the stuff, then visit an off-licence – preferably an independent one, where the staff will know about wine and want to help you match something to what you're eating, rather than talking to some superannuated shelf-stacker in a supermarket who's been told to push the latest wine of the month because they've got too much left over in the warehouse.

And here's what to think about while you're choosing.

APERITIFS
A nice start to the evening. They can be anything from sparkling wine to (if you're feeling generous) champagne; cocktails to gin and tonics. But remember: it's the first drink your guests will be having, so don't view aperitifs as a competition to see how much booze you can sink within the first half hour. Unless you've suddenly realized your dinner's destined to be a disaster, so you want everyone so sloshed they won't remember what anything tastes like.

So be careful with the measures, and if you're going for cocktails, opt for ones that are tasty but not too boozy.

Another thing about cocktails: if you choose to serve them, choose ones that don't need too much preparation – otherwise that's one more thing to worry about when you should be concentrating all your mind on the meal. It's also one more set of kit to buy, adding to the expense of the night. Plus: who really likes a show-off with a shaker? You'll remind them of Tom Cruise in *Cocktail*, and that's bound to annoy one of your guests. Or two. Or three. Or all of them.

WINE
Once you sit down to eat, it's usual to move on to wine. White generally goes with fish and lighter meats like chicken. Red accompanies heavier meat like beef, pork and duck. But for every rule there's an exception: a chicken served with a heavy, spicy sauce would probably need to be paired with a red, whereas chicken with a lighter, smoother jus will be just fine with white.

Once you've decided which colour suits a dish, then the next thing to think about is making sure it matches the food flavours. If you've gone for white, but are serving it with a dish that has a bit of spice in it, then go for a dry white. But if you have a more fruity recipe, then you'll need to lay on something altogether sweeter.

Generally don't serve red before white. So even if you're making a meaty starter, followed by fish, you would probably stick to the white all the way through.

White is best served chilled. That sounds obvious. But in a hot room, it doesn't stay chilled in the glass too long. So serve small amounts – and top up glasses regularly. That way you also get to find out which of your diners know anything about wine: if they demand a full glass, then they don't!

Don't hit your guests with too heavy a wine to start with – otherwise what follows will only feel like a letdown. Start with lighter grapes, then build to a bigger, full-bodied finish with a red, or port – or even a dessert wine, which has an altogether different feel.

In an ideal world, serve white in a smaller glass, and red in a bigger one to let the bouquet breathe. Most of us, though, don't live in an ideal world – so if you're going to change colours midway through the meal, make sure there's plenty of water on the table so your guests can rinse out their glasses.

If you're lucky enough to have servants (or kids who will do the job for an extra bit of pocket money), then they should know to serve the wine on the right. So if they don't they should be sacked. Although of course you can't sack your kids.

Don't boast about how much you spent. Unless you swiftly want to find yourself crossed off one or two guest lists, because people are too afraid to serve you the more humbly priced plonk that they can afford.

PORT
This should be served only when the table is cleared, and generally with a Stilton or cheese course. But that is, of course, tradition, and you can feel free to ignore it. Although we wouldn't recommend port with your main. If you are one of life's traditionalists, then you might want to pass the port – and in a custom that is thought to originate from the British navy, you pass the port to port. For landlubbers that means clockwise, and generally involves the port starting with the host, who serves the person to his or her right, then themselves, before passing it to the guest on the left. That guest then helps themselves, before it's passed on around the table, until it returns to the host. Although if it stops, there is apparently a ritual question and answer involving the Bishop of Norwich which should get it started again. But life really is too short to say anything else other than, 'Please pass the b*****y port!'

BUY ENOUGH

Obvious really. Except for when your guests quaff wine like water. Then you discover they have downed all your drink midway through the main, and all you have left to accompany that blood-red beef is the warm white they brought with them. If it's good wine it won't matter if you over-buy – because you'll have something for another day. As a rule of thumb, allow half a bottle per person per course, plus one extra per dish for luck.

GUESTS' WINE

Finally, there's the age-old question of what to do with wine brought by your guests. Hopefully most of them will think it's a good wine (although there will be one or two skinflints who try to palm off a ropey old vintage to help clear their cellar). So they might be a bit miffed at seeing the choice they've agonized over for ages in the off-licence being slung straight into your wine rack. They don't know you've spent ages mulling over matching wines for the menu (and they don't really want to hear about your extensive knowledge of wine). So massage their feelings by saying what an excellent choice they've made, what an excellent addition it will be to your cellar, and how you'll look forward to drinking it later.

Some contestants go to great lengths to get the freshest possible produce, such as Glasgow winner Paul Lydon, who went fishing for his trout.

things to do in advance to make life easier

A good dinner party is not just about the food – it's about how well the table is set, a good choice of pre-dinner drinks, the right pre-meal nibbles and much more besides. All that takes plenty of planning but can be easily overlooked when it comes to the big day, because you're worrying about the food and only the food.

To make life easier, there are a few simple things you can do well in advance of your dinner party. And by well in advance, we mean three days and not three hours before your guests arrive.

So here's what to do.

Make sure the salt and pepper cellars are filled up. A simple thing to do, but an annoying thing to forget. There'll always be one guest who likes their food tasting like the sea. And it's very annoying to have to get up mid-meal to fill the salt cellar up.

Wash and iron enough napkins.
Whatever you serve, one of your guests will end up with food on their chin, so everyone will need something on hand for spillages. Paper ones, I hear you say? Fine if you want the meal to resemble a children's tea party. However, if your aim is to impress, then the only answer is cloth – and clean cloth napkins at that. So if you haven't got any: go out and buy some. If you have, check they're clean.

Think about what's going on the table. Hopefully a table cloth; preferably a white one, to give a cool, stylish look. So where is it? At the bottom of the laundry basket, probably, with the red wine stain still on it. Time for a wash. Or two. Or three. And if the marks still won't come out, then beg, borrow or steal another one.

Make sure you have enough crockery for all the dishes you're going to cook and serve. It's no good discovering your other half has smashed two of your ramekins and forgot to tell you until you're in the middle of making dessert, when it's far too late to go out and buy replacements.

Check on your cutlery as well. It helps to have enough to go round. Of everything: knife, forks, spoons, the lot. Unless you want your guests to eat with their hands. Which isn't great if you're serving soup. Or very hot food. Or indeed any food at all. Unless it's Indian. Even then someone won't take to the idea of using their hands, so you should always have cutlery available. Assume everyone will want to use a knife and fork. But don't leave them to ask. If you dish up Chinese with chopsticks, you can guarantee that someone won't be able to handle theirs and seems to be eating the rice one grain at a time. However, they'll plough on regardless, too embarrassed to say anything. So unless you like serving dessert at approaching midnight, ensure you have cutlery on the table, so the chopstick-phobe can surreptitiously bring them into play without upsetting you.

Inspect the drinks cabinet and your glassware. We're not just talking about the booze here. Someone will love a gin or vodka and tonic: if you're planning to offer those, check that your only bottle of tonic isn't the one you opened last Christmas and is now flatter than a pancake. Check also that your partner hasn't secretly finished off the last bottle of Gordon's. Think about non-drinkers and make sure you have a decent soft-drinks

option. Even if you're going to serve Eau de Privatized Water Company, then at least have a lemon or lime ready to take off the taste of fluoride. And make sure you've got the right glassware: gin and tonic tumblers, wine glasses, even sherry glasses if your aunt Maud's coming for dinner. And a quick check that there are no lipstick marks left over is usually quite a good idea as well.

Put your beer and wine in the fridge to cool. It's never too early to start, but it's certainly too late when you're thrusting a very warm bottle of Sauvignon Blanc into the freezer as the doorbell announces the arrival of your first guest.

Check the ice tray. Whether it's winter or summer, it's always nice to have the option of serving a cool drink; and once again, if you leave it until an hour before everyone arrives, the chances are your ice tray will be emptier than the coffers of Britain's banks.

Think suitable nibbles. Not too many nuts, because there will always be someone who's one peanut away from casualty. Not too many exotic crisps, with bizarre flavours, unless you don't want your guests to taste their starter. And not too many nibbles full-stop, because you do want your guests to eat the meal, rather than push it aside because they're full of snacks.

Work out a seating plan: who's likely to talk to whom. If you don't think about that until everyone sits down, then before you know it, they've all grabbed their own places, and the two people who really don't want to sit next to each other are left with side-by-side chairs.

Check the toilet. Unless you're planning to whisk them in and out of the house in under an hour, then there will be one room they'll want to visit other than your lounge and dining room: the toilet. A place that's all too easily forgotten. But all too often used. So check there's enough toilet roll. That the soap dispenser's full. And that there's a clean towel hanging up. That way you'll avoid lots of embarrassment all round.

Do a bit of cleaning. The front hall, lounge, dining room – and of course the toilet. A messy hall followed by a scruffy sitting room will hardly inspire confidence among your guests in what is to follow at the dinner table. Don't spit and polish as if the Queen was coming, but do make a bit of an effort.

how to set the perfect table

You can cook the most beautiful food, but if your guests are eating it in terrible surroundings, they'll barely notice. So whatever you do, don't neglect the table. It's not hard to get it right; but it's also not hard to get it badly wrong. So here are a few simple dos and don'ts.

Flowers: avoid large displays. Unless you want your guests to think they're coming to a wedding. Which presumably you don't. They get in the way so people can't see across the table, they're too easily knocked over and there's always the risk of inducing an unwanted bout of hay fever in one of your guests. If you want your table to look nice with some floral decorations, then choose wisely: something that's not stuffed with pollen, and sits low on the table, well out of everyone's eye line. So you'll probably need to invest in a shallow, fairly small vase or clear bowl, and flowers that fit accordingly.

Candles. A nice idea in theory. But …
Think how drunk your guests can get. Then think of the potential when one of them knocks over the candle when you're out of the room. They all sit there waiting for someone else to deal with it. And before you know it the place is filled with smoke, someone's poured a whole water jug followed by a load of red wine onto the flames to put them out, your carpet's soaking and stained, and the whole night's a disaster. So if you want candles, then probably best to go for small, free-standing versions that can sit in their own glass: no taller than a tumbler, with a small flame and any wax can drip straight back into the container. Plus if they are those scented ones that you or your partner loves, they'll hide the smell of any burnt food.

Water for everyone. Particularly useful when one of your guests looks like they're enjoying the wine a little bit too much. Then you can channel their nervous drinking into some sobering H_2O, whilst cunningly placing the bottle of wine at the other end of the table.

Put a jug of water on the table. But fill up everyone's glasses before they sit down. Otherwise, you'll have to get up again as soon as you've sat down because the first round of water will have emptied the jug, and no one likes their host getting up and down like a jack in the box. But make sure it's a jug. Plastic water bottles are for the gym and the office. Not sophisticated soirees.

Napkins. Obvious. Nothing more needs to be said. Apart from they definitely shouldn't be paper. (Paper napkins – and plastic water bottles instead of a jug – are the two things that *Come Dine With Me* contestants often dock points for.) Napkin rings can also add a nice touch. Alternatively, if you're any good with your hands, it always looks impressive to have folded napkins on everyone's plate. As long as they don't collapse while your back's turned, and when you come to seat everyone look like they've been thrown there.

Serving spoons: don't forget these. It's always nice to allow your guests to serve themselves. But it also helps to have enough spoons for them to do so. And if you forget them, that's something else you have to bob up from the table to collect.

Salt and pepper mill. Present only so you can see which of your guests lacks table manners, because they season their food before tasting it. Then you can strike them off the list for your next dinner party. But someone will definitely want to use them, so put them on the table.

Some napkins or pan-holders to manoeuvre hot serving dishes with. Always useful to avoid your guests having to make a trip to casualty for scalds to the hand.

Place names. You've already worked out your seating plan, and you've ensured that the two people who rowed at your last dinner party are at opposite ends of the table this time round, and that those two you reckon will hit it off are next to each other. Place names are an easy way to get the seating as you really want it. Because otherwise, just as you call everyone to table, you'll have to dash back into the kitchen because the rice has just boiled over, and by the time you get back to the dining room, everyone's chosen exactly the chair you didn't want them to.

Presents: as a rule don't. You've gone to all the trouble of cooking your guests dinner, so the only thing they really need to take home with them is a full stomach, and the hope that they won't wake up with a sore head the next day because you're a bit tight and have plied them with cheap plonk all night.

what to do when people arrive

If there's one immutable law of dinner parties, it's that the doorbell will go just when you're in the middle of some vital piece of preparation. A little voice in your head will say, 'Oh, I'll only need another minute, they can wait.' Tell it to shut up because there's nothing worse for a guest than being kept waiting at the door. Except, that is, being kept waiting when it's cold and raining; which it probably will be, even though you haven't noticed because you've been too busy cooking for the last two hours.

Before you go to answer the door, that little annoying voice in your head will also say, 'I can leave the pan on the heat because I'll be back in a moment.' Once again, tell it to shut up. The hustle and bustle of arrivals will mean all thoughts of cooking will go clean out of your mind — until your fire alarm goes off to tell you that it's rather more brûlee than crème you'll be serving.

When you do receive your guests, you're more than likely to confront one of the most awkward conundrums facing any host: what to do about your guests' footwear? The tradition of everyone volunteering to take their shoes off as soon as they walk into someone's house seems to have gone the way of the shilling and the Routemaster bus.

Basically, there are two camps. There's the camp that can't bear shoes in the house: they don't wear shoes in their own home and they wouldn't expect to wear them in yours either. Secondly, there are those who think that if you're going to invite someone to dinner and expect them to dress up, then you shouldn't expect them to take their shoes off, because the shoes are as much a part of their outfit as their shirt — and you wouldn't expect them to take that off. And doubtless your guest has dressed on the basis of keeping their shoes on, so who knows what's underneath?

Your guests will almost certainly fall into one or other category; so, no doubt, will you. With luck, it will be a meeting of minds: your guests might share your no-shoe preference and fling off their footwear as soon as they're through the door. Alternatively, you and they might agree with the idea that shoes are all part of an outfit, so you don't mind if they barge through with their boots on straight into the dining room. Indeed, you'd probably prefer it that way, as the sight of bare feet, or holey socks, is something you thought you'd left behind with school gym lessons.

There also shouldn't be too much trouble when the pro-shoe host invites a guest who falls into the no-shoes-in-the-house camp.

Hopefully, the no-shoes-indoors type will have planned their outfit right down to their socks, which will be clean-smelling and all in one piece, or even toenails, which will be clean, trimmed and possibly even painted.

The real trouble starts for the host who absolutely hates footwear indoors, while his or her guests take the opposite view on the troublesome question. The host has two choices. Option one: grin and bear it as they walk straight on to your carpets. Say to yourself, you don't mind, you're not going to let it spoil your evening. A little bit of dirt doesn't matter …

Option two – likely to come into play if you've just had cream carpets laid – is to ask your guests to take their shoes off. It's a simple sentence really: 'Would you mind awfully taking your shoes off?'

Easy to say – except that acute embarrassment is likely to stop the words coming out. Instead, you and your newly arrived guests will spend ages loitering in the hallway as you stall them, pretending that you need to work out where to hang up coats, asking whether they had a good journey to get here, admiring the wine and flowers they've brought. Eventually, shame-faced, you'll spill out the words and it will sound as if you're lecturing schoolchildren. Then brace yourself for a chorus of awkward 'of course's. Then it's time to hastily avert

your eyes – and possibly even your nose.

If dealing with this social awkwardness isn't bad enough, what about when your partner or flatmate takes the diametrically opposite view? They usher people straight on in without thinking for a moment about the agony they're going to put you through for the rest of the night, as you can't take your eyes off the guests' muddy footwear nestled dirtily in your carpet, or your flatmate's sister's stilettos marching up and down on your soft-wood floor.

So, if you are part of a two-person hosting team, there's only one course of action: agree a shoes policy before the evening starts. And if you've agreed a no-shoe policy, and you're the anti-shoe partner, then volunteer yourself as the meeter and greeter. Because you know your fellow host will cop out and fail to follow through. Especially when they notice what lovely shoes their friends are wearing, and want to see them in the full light of the lounge, rather than the dimly lit hallway.

Once everyone's finally got their stockinged – or still shoed – feet on your shagpile, the next step is fixing a drink. So ask. And listen to the answer. Sounds obvious: but it's classic nervous-host behaviour to ask the question, but be too concerned about where everyone's sat and whether there are enough nibbles to catch anyone's reply. Then you have to ask again, and that looks rude.

Make everyone sit down. That way, when you go to fix them a drink, they cannot follow you into the kitchen and spot just how much you're struggling to keep everything under control. Pass the nibbles – and keep an eye out for greedy guests who colonize the bowl.

Remind the guests who else is coming; you'll have told them, but there's a good chance they'll have forgotten, especially if they don't know them. In that case, fill them in on a few salient facts about them. When the doorbell goes again, get up saying, 'That must Bob and Sarah.' That way they can have no excuse not to remember the names of the other guests.

This time – if you've won the first shoe face-off with your opening guests – the arrival won't be so fraught. As the second round of invitees come in and start taking any coats off, you can avoid the shoe conundrum by announcing 'Rachel and John are here, as you can see by their shoes.'

If that hint passes straight over the tops of their heads, then try, 'There's plenty of room to leave your shoes next to theirs.' If your dumb diners miss even that obvious hint, then it will have to be another, 'Do you mind taking your shoes off?' But try not to do it in your most demented Basil Fawlty voice.

Once you've safely negotiated your guests through the hallway into the sitting room, it's time for introductions. This is

The lowest ever scorer on *Come Dine With Me* achieved a dismal 9 points in all, an average score of 2.25.

where true Britishness comes into play, and you, as a host, will be tempted to mutter very quickly, 'BobthisisJohnRachelJohnthisis BobandSarah.' So by the time you've finished your new guests think they're dining with Bobbing Sir.

Take the time to introduce everyone slowly and pause in between so they can repeat each other's names, which will at least give them a 50–50 chance of remembering them. Unless they're a boy, when it's more like 20–80 against.

Ask them what they want to drink. But don't, whatever you do, say: 'I know Rachel and John from university, and they live in Clapham; while Bob and Sue are work friends who live in Wandsworth.' Unless you want to guarantee complete silence while you're in the kitchen sorting out the aperitifs. Because most people have only two questions up their sleeve when they meet strangers: 'How do you know our mutual friend?' and 'Have you had far to come?' (There is, of course, the weather, but stating the obvious about the climate is not guaranteed to get the chat flowing.) Of course, there will be some guests who have more to say than that: inappropriate things about what people are wearing, or how much older someone is than they expected. But hopefully they're not the guests you've invited, because your friends are a lot more cultured than that.

If you're ambitious and have decided to cater for more than four guests, you'll have to go through all this again when your next set of guests arrive. With double the number of introductions to make, it's more important than ever that you say everything slowly and clearly.

After that it's a question of allowing a suitable amount of time with your diners before you call them to the table. But don't leave that to the very last minute when you're already dishing up as you're guaranteed that someone will want to use the loo. And if you only have one toilet, it will be certain that at least two people will want to go. So if you dish up your soup before telling everyone it's ready, then you can bet it will be almost cold by the time everyone has finally sat down.

ten most common kitchen cock-ups

They're the most common disaster zones, but it's interesting to note – as you'll see when you look through the recipes – how often the winners have ignored the golden rules and triumphed anyway. On your own head be it …

ONE RISOTTO

OK, it's a restaurant favourite that people love to order. But that's because they're not dining with the person who's cooking it, so won't notice the chef's absence. Unlike at a dinner party. However much preparation you do, a risotto is going to mean lots of work that can only be done at the last minute. So you'll be away from the table for a long time: which means lots of stress, because you're worrying what your guests are doing in your absence. It's not an impossible choice, but it's a very brave and risky one: think long and hard before doing it. Then think again. And hopefully decide not to. But if you do, good luck.

TWO POTATOES

Fine to peel them in advance. But only if you put them in water. And definitely don't grate them in advance for rostis, because they'll invariably end up a grey-brown stodgy mess, neither appetizing nor tasty.

THREE AVOCADO

Can be used to make lovely, tasty accompanying dishes. But beware, if they're not done properly, they can turn, in the words of one *Come Dine With Me* guest, into something resembling dog poo. Yes, avocado without the proper treatment can go very brown and unpleasant indeed. The best thing to do is put some lemon or lime juice into it: the citric acid helps stop it going off.

FOUR STEAK

It's a great idea. Until one of your guests wants it rare, another medium rare, and a third well done. So you have to juggle all sorts of different timings. And then by the time you get everything to the table, you've given the rare to the blood-phobic diner and the well done to the carnivore who loves his meat gory. So one's groaning, and the other's fainting. And neither is particularly keen to swap with the other once the mistake's been discovered. So think hard about doing this, and have a plan to ensure the gore-hunt gets his pink meat, and your faint-hearted diner enjoys his cremated fillet.

FIVE SOUFFLÉS

There's a reason why Gordon Ramsay got people to cook soufflés in *Hell's Kitchen*. Because they're very, very difficult. Even for professionals. Let alone amateurs who come to tackle them after slaving away on a starter and main, downing a few glasses of wine, and generally playing the stressed host.

SIX PACKAGING

Make sure you remove it all. There's always that tricky little bit of cotton-wool type material that sits at the bottom of a joint of meat, for example. Fail to spot it, and you'll be serving up beef *à la plastic*, and your friends will be mysteriously busy every time you try to invite them round to dinner.

SEVEN NEW OVENS

Know how they work. It sounds obvious – but it's all too easy to forget in the effort to sort everything else out. If you've just moved into a place, or you've just had a new oven fitted, then take a bit of time to check out how it works – or indeed whether it works at all. Thinking your main is roasting away when all it's doing is enjoying a blast of cold air from your unheated fan spells ruin for your timings, and your evening.

EIGHT COOKING IN FRONT OF YOUR GUESTS

You have a kitchen-diner. Perfect for playing host – even if you have to be at the stove, you can eavesdrop on the sparkling conversation and throw in the odd comment while stirring the sauce. Perfect, that is, until you start to feel performance pressure. And then the conversation dries up anyway. Because they're watching you. Plus they can smell burning, so they're wondering just what they're going to have to eat and are trying to work out whether it really is all going terribly wrong. Plus they are eating in a place that looks like it's been hit by a small hurricane because you haven't had time to wash up. So at least allow yourself extra time in your day to clear up if there's no door you can close to hide the mess. And try not to burn anything.

NINE PETS

Banish them. Because you can guarantee that when your back's turned little Tiddles the cat will be taking a shine to your tasty hors d'oeuvres, so you'll have to chuck them away. Or worse still, your guests will discover a stray hair in their food. And sadly, much as you'd want it to, the ground won't open up to swallow you at that moment. Instead, you'll just have to plough on gamely until the end of your dinner party, watching your guests gingerly picking their way through the food trying to make sure they're not about to munch on another unwanted little morsel.

TEN DISHING UP

You don't need to be Einstein to realize that hot food hitting cool china will soon become a cold, congealed mess that your diners would rather you hadn't served. So warm your plates and your serving dishes. It's another thing that's all too easily overlooked. And don't, whatever you do, spend ten minutes counting how many carrots you've dished out on each plate. You'll be counting all over again when you come to clear away as your diners will have passed on the tepid objects.

Entertainment laid on for guests by contestants on *Come Dine With Me* has included belly dancers, fake paparazzi, poetry readings and singing.

how to choose the starter

The starter is possibly THE most important part of the meal. A good first course and you set the tone for the evening; it puts your guests at ease and they can more easily forgive any faux pas that might follow. A bad beginning and your confidence will be shattered, along with that of your guests, who will be nervously eyeing their watches wondering when this culinary catastrophe is going to end.

And it's not just about the taste. Too much starter and there's no room for the riches that might follow; too little and your guests will bolt the rest of the meal rather than enjoy it because they're starving. Too spicy and even the most delicious dessert will still taste of chilli because the guests' mouths have yet to recover. Too bland and no one's appetite will be whetted for what follows.

But the most important thing to consider when choosing a starter is whether it can be prepared in advance. If there's one dish you should try to have ready before your guests arrive, it's the first course. An opener that takes all your time and attention just when your guests have arrived means you can't do all the things you need to do to get a dinner party off the ground: sorting drinks, introducing everyone and generally breaking the ice, so that all your invitees settle in comfortably for the evening.

So choose wisely, so that as much as possible is done in advance and you play the perfect host when your guests arrive. Then,

after a suitable interval, and with you barely absent, you can serve them their first course. Once they've enjoyed their starter, downed a drink or two and got to know each other a bit more, then everyone will forgive you if you have to spend more time in the kitchen to do the main course. But if you've already been absent preparing the first course, and the guests are beginning to wonder who exactly it is who's invited them this evening, then you've got off on the wrong foot.

That's not to say every starter has to be cold: a swiftly warmed soup, speedily cooked scallops on a salad, even fast-fried octopus can work well as you'll be in and out of the kitchen in no time. As long, that is, as you've got everything else ready on the table: bread, water, dishes all set out with the base of salad, so that you're only cooking one thing – and you don't have to jump up from the table as soon as you've sat down. Of course, if there's two of you hosting, one can handle the guests while the other does the starter – while hopefully not being absent too long.

how to choose the main course

The main course doesn't get its name by chance: it is the main thing your guests will be eating – or at least you hope it is, if everything goes to plan. So it needs to be sizeable enough to be satisfying, tasty enough to be talked about afterwards by your guests and craftily chosen to complement your starter.

As it's the biggest, it's also the dish that needs the most work – so if you want to be the host who's always at the table, you'll have to opt for something you can do as much as possible in advance – then stick in the oven the right amount of time before serving. If you have a co-host, or you can trust your guests to entertain themselves, then you have more freedom to opt for something that can see you closeted in the kitchen for half an hour or more.

If you go for meat, then bear in mind that not all meat eaters are perhaps as carnivorous as you: they might love chicken, but have a problem with red meat for health reasons. They might pig out on pork but think veal isn't the real deal because of the way it's produced. So don't assume all meat-eaters will be happy with everything.

Then there's the tricky decision of how to cater for the vegetarian.

You have two options: either base your meal entirely round their tastes; or do two different options: one meat and one meat-free (or meat- and fish-free).

Option one is the easier. But it's probably not going to make the majority of your diners happy. Vegetarian restaurants are in a minority for a reason: most meat-eaters don't really like eating veggie food. And the same probably applies when they go round to your house. They'll admire you for trying but won't exactly be putting you head of the guest list for their next dinner. You'll also be cooking veggie food, which you might not have done before, for everyone. While the vegetarian will probably forgive you as you've made an effort for them, the meat-eaters will go home cursing you not only for dismissing their animal cravings, but also for serving a pretty poor veggie substitute as well.

Option two is obviously the trickier one, as you have to do two dishes. So twice as many timings to juggle. Twice as many things that can go wrong. But you'll have potentially twice the number of satisfied guests. Your carnivores get their daily helping of blood and guts. The vegetarian will be impressed that you made a special effort for them. The only disadvantage is that you'll probably be top of their list as a guest at their next dinner party, where you'll get to find out all about the joys of tofu.

There is, of course, a third option: cook what you want to eat, i.e. meat and lots of it, and let them have the vegetables. But that's not really an option if you want still them to be your friend. Or you've cooked most of the vegetables in meat fat. Or both.

Then there's the question of what to do if one of your guests is a pescetarian. The obvious answer would seem to be to cook fish. But beware: that can be the road to ruin. Fish is the main-course equivalent of Marmite for many people: they either love it or hate it. Most of us can pretty much stomach a lentil, vegetable and pine-nut bake – life-threatening nut allergies aside. Stick a piece of fish in front of half the population, however, and if it's not covered in batter, you'll have plenty left over to feed the cat. Plus the iron law of cooking is that while one person loves white fish, they'll hate seafood, while the seafood lover will loathe that oven-baked sea bream. So check, double check and triple check everyone's tastes before dashing in to cook fish – they'll thank you for it when they get to eat food they like.

Whatever you opt for, if your main dish needs lots of cooking at the last minute, then don't forget you need to eat your starter too. Until then, you can't do anything – so the time between the end of the starter and main will be at least as long as the prep and cooking time of the second course; and possibly longer, as there's a chance that something will go wrong. So before choosing a main course that needs lots of last-minute cooking, think whether you're going to be happy leaving your guests unattended, and whether they'll mind a long wait between courses. Probably not if you've cooked a relatively heavy starter, but if you haven't, they might not appreciate a long pause.

Choosing a main course, though, isn't just about the central recipe. It's also about what goes alongside it: the side dishes. Most of your guests won't be expecting to be served as if they're at some fancy restaurant which charges an arm and a leg for a tiny bit of meat, on top of an even smaller amount of veg, sitting in the middle of a vast sea of china. Instead, they'll be looking for some tasty vegetables to both fill them up and complement the main course. So think just as long and hard about your side dishes as your main. And don't forget the sort of classics you prepare ahead of time and just pop in the oven – potatoes dauphinoise, for instance.

how to choose the dessert

Hurrah, we hear the tired dinner-party host say, we've finally got on to dessert. The main and starter were great, so a quick bowl of fruit salad will be fine. Prepared loads in advance, so you can start to get slowly sozzled once you've plonked the main course plates on the table. Wrong. Wrong. Wrong. And wrong again.

The dessert is the last thing your guests will eat. It will be the final memory they take away of the evening. If that memory is of a fruit salad that's got slightly fizzy because you've left it out in the heat too long, accompanied by some ropey-looking cream, that's how they'll remember your dinner party: a bit ropey. So give dessert some thought. Indeed as much thought as the other two courses, so that all the good work you've done up until then is not wasted.

The most effortless – but nevertheless just as tasty – option is to go for a prepared-ahead dessert that can be in the fridge (or freezer) until it's needed. Then it will miraculously appear before the diners, looking like something off the dessert trolley at one of their favourite restaurants, with you hardly having broken sweat. Sounds easy, and can be, if – and this is a big if – you get the planning spot on to allow enough time for something to set, cool or freeze. Make your pannacotta too late and it will come out looking more like thick double cream than a prime Italian dessert. Like any other dish, if not more so, dessert needs near perfect planning – or enough drink to ply the guests with between main and dessert, while you play for time to allow the dish to finally set.

A hot dish, of course, requires cooking at the last minute – and that means extra work at the end of the dinner party. Easy, we hear you say: the whole thing will be a breeze.

But before you confidently embark on that complicated warm dessert, think about how tired you'll be at the end of the evening. If you can't imagine that, then remember you could be standing on your feet for four hours, dashing in and out serving people food. If you can't imagine how exhausted that might make you, then think about running around after small children all afternoon – and that's how tired you'll probably be. If that fills you with horror, then hot afters are probably not for you. However, if you can cope with running around after small children all afternoon – then crack on with a warm dessert. Because it can be a show-stopping way to finish the evening, as most people generally take the safe route with a chilled one. (Of course, you can opt for a hot dessert – like the classic chocolate fondants – that can be prepared ahead, then whacked in the oven and dished up within minutes to make it look as if you are the equivalent of Mother Teresa when it comes to miracle puds.)

Then, of course, there's the ultimate show-stopper, the hot dessert prepared in front of the guests, like crêpes Suzette. You need the kit, you need the chutzpah, and you need no fear of failure – because flambéing is tricky, with the risk of either falling flat or singeing your eyebrows.

So good luck and happy puds.

There have been seven occasions when there were joint winners – with the prize money being shared between them.

how to be the perfect host at the table

The theme of this book is hosting a dinner party. Not just cooking one. For one simple reason: you are playing host, and not just cook. Someone who cooks a dinner party spends all their time worrying about the food; they're missing in action almost all the time in the kitchen, and when they're finally sat down, their mind's on the next course, so they don't notice everyone's eating in silence, their glasses are empty and the atmosphere would make a wake look like a knees-up.

Someone who hosts a dinner party not only lays on a sumptuous three-course meal, they make the evening one to remember by ensuring that everyone is having a good time as well as eating a good dinner. There are a few simple things you can do to ensure your evening is remembered for all the right reasons.

Reusing glasses. If you're reading this, the chances are that you won't have a collection of cut glass that would put Pilkingtons to shame. So you'll need to think about how you optimize your tumblers if you've served gin and tonics. In very polite society, it would be rude to ask people to reuse their glasses for water. But if you're short on the glass front – and with friends – then feel free to ask your guests to retain what they were given for their G&T to use at the table for water.

Be attentive. Six empty glasses at a dinner for six are a sign of a host who's spending too much time talking – or cooking – and not enough time topping up the drinks.

Watch out for the nervous guest who glugs down too much. Your best friend's new partner will be understandably nervous about meeting a load of strangers. So it'll be no surprise when they hit the drink, and turn from meek and mild to slurring or even snoring. You'll soon notice when someone's drinking too much – when theirs is the first glass that's empty. To avoid a scene, fill other people's glasses, leaving just a drop in the bottom, which you then pour into the glugger's glass, saying, 'I'll just get another bottle.' Then take time out before uncorking the next one, so they'll have to drink some water.

Then, if all else fails, ask your best friend to help clear the plates, and have a subtle word in the kitchen: they'll be desperate for their new date not to embarrass themselves in front of your friends, so will take the hint to help them curb the drinking. Or, if they don't care, then the relationship's not destined to last – in which case, don't worry about what state the new girlfriend or boyfriend gets into, as their behaviour will keep you amused for long after they've been given the heave-ho.

Remember your diners' names. If you persist on calling one of your diners Diana when her name's Deborah, then the nicest food in the world isn't going to take the sour taste out of her mouth. If you're the sort of person who immediately forgets someone's name as soon as they say it (i.e. you're a male of the species), repeat it out loud immediately, and then say it again, so it might actually stick.

Keep the conversation going – for more on this, see page 52.

Keep the conversation going – for more on this, see page 52.

Plating up the main: serving dishes versus serving up. This is a big conundrum for any host. Serving up in the kitchen and giving everyone their meal on a plate takes the hassle out of sitting at the table. But it also risks giving everyone too much or – worse still – too little to eat. Also, if you spend too long making everything look pretty, then the food's cold before you get it to the table. Serving dishes solve both those problems, but you need to ensure that everyone gets

to them before the greedy boys have snaffled the best bits. They also need to get around the table quick enough to ensure that someone isn't left staring at a selection of rather cold carrots and lukewarm spuds: not always easy when everyone is so polite that they're waiting for everyone else to serve. themselves. In which instance, you'll probably have to take charge, and then you'll look like the superintendent in *Oliver Twist*. Neither way is perfect, but whichever way you go, bear the potential pitfalls in mind.

Dealing with smokers. One of the trickiest hosting conundrums. A smoker loves to finish off a meal with a good puff. But these days, fewer and fewer people accept it – and you might not the next day either, when your curtains smell like they've been dipped in an ash-tray. So check out if anyone's a smoker in advance. Then make some sort of arrangement for them to smoke somewhere – in a porch if you've got one, even under a gazebo if you have the time and inclination. Alternatively, you could just tell them they have a really dirty habit and should give it up, so they're not smoking anywhere near your house. But you'll probably need to be half cut to do that – which doesn't really gel with the goal of being the perfect host. Of course, if you're the host and a smoker, then you'll be desperate to light up inside. Unfortunately, there will invariably be one guest who doesn't like it. As so often, there are two schools of thought. There's the brave one: it's my house, I'll do what I like in it, and if you don't like it you can disappear before your pudding. Frank, honest – but likely to mean you'll have a couple of desserts left over to eat for breakfast, after two chairs are swiftly vacated. Secondly, there's the option of disappearing outside. Great if there are others who can smoke with you, so you can keep the party going. Sadly, it's not so good if you're all alone – who knows what anarchy will have broken out at the table while you're outside feeding your craving.

Clearing up the plates. No one likes to sit with dirty plates in front of them. Equally, your diners don't want their cutlery whipped from under them the moment they have put their knife and fork down, and while they're chewing their last mouthful of food. So allow a suitable time for people to have properly digested each dish without their having to sit in front of a congealing plate of leftovers. This rule applies even if you are dining with the meticulous masticator who is so desperate to avoid dyspepsia he or she chews every mouthful ten times, before swallowing slowly and pausing between bites. When it comes to clearing, whatever you do, don't stack plates if you can avoid it. That means

The highest ever scorer on *Come Dine With Me* is Ian Cook from Liverpool. He scored 39 out of 40, missing out on the perfect score because he put the water on the table in plastic bottles.

your guests will end up passing an ever growing pile of rather dirty crockery and cutlery between them, while a gravy-smeared knife slides off the top of the stack and into someone's lap: usually belonging to a lady wearing a light-coloured skirt that provides the perfect back-drop for displaying congealed sauce.

Offers of help from guests: politely, but firmly, refuse. Not least because you don't want them to see what a bombsite your kitchen is. So seat those most likely to offer help in the most inaccessible seats at your table, so you can say, 'Oh you are a darling, but you really are pinned in there where you're sat, so don't trouble yourself.' Seat yourself at a suitable chair so you can make a quick exit between courses – and ensure that the lazy guests who are unlikely to raise a finger all night (generally boys) are in the other easy-to-get-to chairs.

Retiring. At some point during the course of the evening, you'll want to retire to somewhere more comfortable. Post-dessert and before coffee or tea is probably a good idea, as by this time you'll have been getting up and down from the table quite a lot, so if you get up again while the others are still seated, they'll start to feel a bit awkward. So taking tea and coffee orders can be a good cue for retiring to the lounge – it allows you to get up with everyone else, and then go to the kitchen to make the hot drinks.

One last thing: as your guests leave, don't forget to thank them for coming. They might not have made quite as much effort as you, but at least they did make the effort of getting there.

dinner party etiquette for guests
(doing the right or wrong thing at the table)

It's time to dine. Everyone's sat at the table. The food's cooked. The drinks are ready to pour. There's just one problem: your guests are apparently frozen motionless in their seats – because they're just not sure about the right etiquette.

We've all been there. That moment at an immaculately set table where you don't know whether your bread plate is the one on the left or right. Where you can't remember if the white wine goes in the small or large glass. Or whether you should serve yourself, serve others, or just wait your turn. And almost all of us have made the wrong move: reaching for the wine at the same time as someone else and nearly knocking it over. Picking up the wrong bread roll, so that the rest of the table is out of kilter.

So here are some simple rules about basic etiquette for guests.

Find out your arrival time. If your host says 7 for 7.30 – then ask them what they think that means: that might sound rude, but everyone has a different idea of 7 for 7.30. Some think that you can turn up any time between 7 and 7.30 because no food will be served until 8 p.m. Others think you should turn up between 7 and 7.10 because dinner will start at 7.30. So the easiest thing is to ask: what time do you want us there. And if your host says 7 for 7.30, reply, so we'll see you just after 7. Then it's up to them to clarify.

So what time should you actually arrive? Your host has said 7 p.m., but they're not expecting the doorbell to go as Big Ben chimes for the seventh time. But they're not expecting you there at 7.30 either. The polite arrival is really between five and ten minutes – but not much more – after the scheduled time. If you are early because of your transport – and it's absolutely freezing outside – then turning up five minutes before the hour is fine, but don't push it much more unless you want an extremely stressed-out host on your hands – or one who's forgotten to do up his flies because he had to jump out of the shower when you knocked.

When you come to sit down for dinner, tradition says that you should serve the lady sitting to the right of the host first – then the other ladies in a clockwise direction, followed by the men. But it's also traditional not to sit around waiting for the food to get cold because you've passed the same serving bowl around the table twice before everyone's taken what they want. So unless you're dining with the Queen, just be polite, and help to serve those around you rather than shovelling your own food onto your plate then putting the serving bowl back on the table.

If it's one of those tables with lots of cutlery, then there's a simple rule: work your way from the outside in. Unless you're being served soup and the first piece of cutlery is a fork. In which case, your host has probably set the table all wrong. So grab the dessertspoon and slurp away, hoping that no one will notice. Then make sure your last mouthful leaves it clean, and sneak it back into its original place.

Remember: liquids on the right, solids on the left – and you'll never drink out of anyone else's wine glass again, or munch their bread by mistake.

Buttering bread: don't just keep dipping your knife in the butter and then smearing it on your bread; if you do that, the butter will resemble a furry ball of crumbs before long. Instead, pick a bit out with your knife, put it on the side of your plate, and then butter your bread from there. If you run out, then repeat the same, after wiping your knife carefully on the bread to remove the crumbs.

Wait until everyone else is served before starting to eat – unless your host tells you otherwise. Even then, think twice about digging in, because they're probably only being polite, and there's bound to be someone who's a bit slow serving themselves, or has nipped to the loo, and you don't want to finish your dinner when someone else is only a few mouthfuls into theirs. Unless you're really greedy and want to grab seconds before everyone else. In which case, everyone will be talking about just how rude you are when you get home. So don't – unless you like people being rude about you.

Try to avoid picking food out of your teeth with your fingers. Toothpicks are now rather out of fashion, so if you really must get rid of the nuisance, retreat decorously to the bathroom before sticking digit to molar.

If you want something on the table but it's the other side of someone else's plate, think before reaching over for it: after all, would you want someone's bracelet dangling on your dinner? Instead, just ask. But only ask if the person next to you isn't talking – although if they don't stop talking and you're absolutely desperate for it, then try to catch someone else's eye and ask them to pass it.

Never lick or put your knife in your mouth.

Forks. They're called forks for a simple reason: to fork up food. Not spoon it up. Otherwise, they'd be called spoons. So forks shouldn't be turned over and used like spoons, unless you're eating peas, sweetcorn, rice or other similar foods – and in that instance, you should hold the fork with your right hand.

Don't eat with your mouth open. Even if you've got a cold and it means you can barely breathe. Go blue in the face rather than show a mouthful of half-chewed food.

It's fine to serve yourself with drinks – but it's more polite to offer the bottle to the people sat either side of you first.

Napkins. You're not a baby, so they don't get tucked into your collar.

Don't use your napkin as a handkerchief. Even if your nose is running because you're eating the hottest curry you've ever come across, you must resist the temptation to blow your nose with it. It's for dabbing at food stains, and dabbing alone. If you absolutely must blow your nose, then use a tissue, or, for want of that, retreat to the bathroom.

Compliment your host on their food. Even if it's horrible. But if it is horrible, don't go over the top. Even the most deluded cook will spot something's up when people gush ridiculously over charred chicken.

Try to eat what you're given. Leaving food looks rude, no matter what. If you've been given too much to start with, then ask for a smaller portion, or give some away: there will always be someone at the table with a bigger appetite than you and they'll be delighted to finish your plate. That way, you're happy, they're happy and your host's happy when they come to clear empty plates from the table.

If you've taken too much and can't eat it, then apologize by saying something like 'My eyes are bigger than my stomach', and pray that the massive guy on the other side of the table isn't seething because he hasn't had enough to eat, while you've grabbed too much. Mezze platters to share mean what they say: to share. That means equal amounts for everyone, not you scoffing half of it because you eat three times faster than everyone else. If you don't do it but your partner does, then subtly pick up the plate when they've taken their share before they can dig in their fork again, and pass it to the other end of the table. If they say they want some more, just say, 'Oh dear, your maths is so bad, isn't it? There are twelve chicken satay, and four of us, so that's three each and you've had yours already. I suppose adding up never has been your strong point.' That way they won't be able to complain or ask for more. And you won't leave your host in an embarrassing position.

If you are that massive guy on the other side of the table who wants that extra food that someone has left behind, don't just take it off the plate. Or even ask for it. Just sit there in silence, and remember, when you have a dinner party, not to invite Mr Selfish.

When you've finished eating, put your knife and fork together facing away from you, so that you let everyone else know you're done.

how to be the perfect guest

So that's how to be the perfect diner when it comes to dinner party etiquette. But there's actually more to being a good guest than knowing how to butter your bread, or where your bread knife should go. Your etiquette might be perfect, but if you're a bit tight, bore the pants off the other guests or try to upstage your host, then you're not likely to get a lot of invites in the future.

So here are a few little tips on what to do to ensure you're the person who gets invited back again, and again, and again – and preferably because you're great company, rather than because your mates enjoy a good laugh because you're such an unwittingly entertaining drunk.

Bring a bottle of wine (or if you don't drink, some chocolates). Or two, if you drink like a fish. Turning up empty-handed, eating like a horse, drinking the place dry and then leaving is a sure-fire route to one thing: lots of nights at home, because your mates cannot be bothered to invite you round any more. They'll soon be sick of doing all the hard work for you and getting nothing in return. So don't be mean.

Don't be tight with what you buy. Walking in with a dusty bottle of £2.99 wine from the local offie isn't good form. If it's the only thing you can lay your hands on, then at least make sure you take the price tag off and brush the bottle free of dust.

Equally, if you bring in a very expensive bottle of wine, don't be upset if your host doesn't open it. Just sit back in the knowledge that you know more about wine than they do. Glug down their cheap plonk, and make sure you wash it down with plenty of water so you don't have a sore head the next day.

What to wear. Don't try to upstage the host. But don't wander in looking like you've just got out of bed, either.

Don't hit on the host's partner while the host is slaving away in the kitchen. Enough said.

Don't drink too much. Sounds obvious. But there will always be someone who gets drunk and embarrasses themselves. It helps for your own sake that it's not you.

Don't outstay your welcome. If the last time you saw your host was twenty minutes ago, and all you've heard since then is the sound of a dishwasher being loaded or pans being scrubbed, then you've probably been hanging around an hour longer than you should have done. Think about when you'd want people to go if it was your party – then knock off half an hour – and that's the time you should be saying your goodbyes.

Don't forget to thank your hosts properly before leaving. Even if it comes out completely slurred. They'll at least admire you for trying to make the effort – even if they only work out what you were trying to say after you've gone.

Send a thank-you note. Your hosts have gone to a lot of trouble for you, so it doesn't take much to send them a card thanking them in return. But be prompt: any later

than a week after the party, and you might as well not have bothered.

And finally: return the favour. If someone invites you to dinner, invite them back. Eventually. Not being much of a cook is not an excuse for failing to return the favour of hospitality: unless, like the empty-handed guest, you're hell-bent on becoming Billy No Mates. Even if you're not much of a cook, try at least to have some sort of supper party for the people who've invited you round in the past. Warn them in advance not to expect much, but at least try: it's the thought that counts, and your friends will love you all the more for it. Unless you're such a bad cook you're bound to give them food poisoning. But even then, there's always Marks and Spencer's …

Come Dine With Me has featured vegans, vegetarians, pescatarians and full-blown carnivores. No vegetarian cook has won outright, but Sue Thomas from Swansea and Tanya Jay from Kent have shared the prize money.

keeping the conversation going

A good dinner party is not just about food. It's also about the conversation – the one thing the host does not have complete control over. Hopefully, by choosing the right combination of people, you'll ensure the conversation flows. But that doesn't always guarantee an endless supply of sparkling repartee. So it's worth thinking about what people can talk about – and where you should seat them to ensure you enjoy convivial chat rather than torrents of tirades.

There will be as many types of dinner-party conversationalists as there are names on your guest list. Ensuring the conversation flows properly will depend on how you handle each of these different types:

DINNER PARTY TYPES
• **The listener**: does exactly what it says on the tin. Quiet, unobtrusive – keeps the conversation going with timely questions. Nods a lot. Happy in their own skin.

• **The listening comic**: similar to the listener, nods and doesn't say a lot, but when he/she does it has the table in hysterics. Happy in their own skin and will leave the dinner party feeling content if they've prompted a few belly laughs during the course of the evening. The only person they really wind up is the listener, who wishes he/she was as funny.

• **The compulsive talker**: he/she can't bear a silence and will talk about anything. Even the quality of the butter if the conversation

is flagging that badly. They're the species of guest who will tend to irritate. So watch out for them: if they're talking too much, then interject to switch the conversation onto something and someone else.

• **The conversation-hogger**, who always manages to turn any chat around to themselves. If you've climbed a mountain, they'll have climbed one higher. If you had a funny meeting with someone famous, they'll have had a funnier one with someone even more famous. They'll always have done something bigger, better or further. And they'll always want to tell everyone about it. (And possibly unveil the T-shirt to go with it.)

• **The big pals**: they only seem to meet up at your place, so they'll be huddled in the corner of the table exchanging stories about things or people no one else knows or cares about – often to the exclusion of the people either side of them. The simple way to handle them is to put them at different ends of the table. They'll still manage to gravitate towards each other at some point during the evening – swapping seats over dessert perhaps – but at least they'll have had to talk to someone else before that.

• **The controversialist** – the sort of person that TV producers love, and book for discussion programmes: they'll say anything to get a reaction. Even if it's the opposite of what they really believe – or even said ten minutes earlier. They love a heated debate, and will stir one up. Great to keep the conversation going, but have to be handled with care: if they overstep the mark and are a bit too provocative, you could have trouble on your hands.

• **The angry young man or woman**: passionate and strong-willed, they have firmly held views on a variety of matters and aren't shy of sharing them with everyone – but simply cannot understand why anyone else would hold the contrary view. Often to be heard saying, 'Look, you're just not listening to what I'm saying,' to someone with the opposing point of view, when actually it's them who's not listening. The combination of controversialist and angry young man or woman will guarantee an exciting night – but can also end in the sort of stand-off that would delight Jerry Springer.

AND HOW TO HANDLE THEM
When it comes to doing your seating plan and handling the conversation, there are a few simple rules to keep the chat going – but not let it get out of hand.

• Don't seat the controversialist next to the angry young man/woman. Unless you want everything to end in tears.

• If there's a conversation-hogger, you're never going to convert them, so put them next to a listener. Or better still a comic listener, so they'll be forced to take a break from talking while everyone else is laughing.

• It doesn't really matter where the compulsive talker sits as they'll always have something to say to someone.

• As already noted, keep the best pals apart.

• Also keep spouses apart, because they can fall into the best-pals camp. Either that or they're not talking anyway because one's in a sulk over something.

• Don't group together too many people who work in the same place.

• Finally, if you can, break up the men and the women.

what to talk about

The old saying has it that there are two things you shouldn't talk about at the table – politics and religion. Actually, there are two far worse things, which you should avoid at all costs: the weather and work. We all experience the same weather, and we all have the same view on it: it's rubbish and we wish it were better. Nothing more to be said. So don't bring it up. And if someone else does, quickly move on to something else.

Work is not much better. It's generally of interest only to you and no one else at the table, unless there are other guests there you work with. But even then that's not a good enough reason for talking about it: because there will always be others at the party who don't have a clue who or what you're talking about – and have even less desire to listen to you discussing it.

Naturally, people you haven't seen for a while will ask how your work's going, but always treat that as a polite inquiry, to be dealt with briefly but informatively, before moving the conversation swiftly on. Unless of course you're a film star, and everyone else around the table is desperate to know what it's like being a film star – then talk as much as you like. But if you're reading this book, you're doubtless having to cook your own meal, rather than get in caterers, so it probably means you're not a film star. Or if you are, you're mighty nice to do it all yourself.

So what of religion and politics? To discuss or not to discuss? Well, it would be a pretty sad world if none of us took any interest in either – and couldn't express our opinion on both. But that's not to say you should definitely bring it up. First, think about whether there's someone at the table with extreme and evangelical views on either subject. If you reckon you've got one of those, steer clear of religion or politics. But if you're an extremist-free zone, then either or both can make for perfectly good conversation. As long as you don't go on too long.

For the rest, here are some simple rules.

Have topics on hand. Controversial new movies; recent headline news; odd celebrity stories: all will be useful if the chat flags. But make sure it's mainstream – asking everyone what they thought of the arthouse Brazilian film you saw in the back room of your local cinema last month will probably fall flat.

Be positive and interesting. Chatting about the new killer bug that's sweeping the local hospital will only have your guests looking for a swift exit. If it does slip into gloom and doom, it's your job as host to bring back the fun.

Listen. If someone's said something, but is a bit shy about saying more, then draw them out. Many people are full of good stories, but need to be encouraged to tell them – while those who want to talk most are often those who don't really have much to say. So if someone's chipped in with something you're intrigued by, don't hesitate to ask for more.

Include everyone. If someone is not talking, it's your job to give them a chance. Ask them for their opinion on what everyone's talking about, and have a handy follow-up question to encourage them to say more.

Moderate, don't dominate. Think of yourself like the anchor on *Have I Got News For You*. Your role is to chip in every so often with a witticism, all the while ensuring that some people don't talk too much and others aren't left out.

Be enthusiastic. If you can't muster a bit of joie de vivre over what everyone's talking about, then don't expect your guests to.

Know your guests. Also, to help ensure everyone's involved, have a few thoughts up your sleeve for leading questions you can ask of your guests, to get them talking about things they've done recently which might then spark another conversation.

If in doubt, make it up. If you're stuck for something to say or a view, then busk it: make up your opinions with a bit of bluff. Hopefully, no one else will be an expert on the subject so they won't notice – and you'll manage to keep everyone interested around the table; then by tomorrow everyone will have forgotten all about it.

Embarrassing: never use the word. Never begin a conversation by asking, 'What's your most embarrassing date/job/moment …' etc. Because everyone's embarrassment threshold will be different – and one of your guests will think it's a great idea to toe-curlingly describe a date that turned into a sexual encounter that went horribly wrong. Sadly only he will think it's a great story. Everyone else will be stunned into silence – except you, who will be bravely trying to shut him up, only to find that he's like the *Titanic* heading unstoppably for the iceberg.

Create a diversion if necessary. Watch the conversation – if it's getting too heated, or drifting in a direction you don't want it to go, then create a diversion by asking if people want more wine, clearing plates, offering to make coffee – or suggesting that everyone leaves the table for comfier seats if you're at the end of the meal. Any of these is likely to take the heat out of a debate.

top ten biggest dinner party disasters

Some of the hosting hiccups that have hit the hopes of our hosts on *Come Dine With Me*. In no particular order.

ONE
Dawn Barry was so overcome with tiredness during her dinner party in Preston that she went for a lie-down and fell asleep. That left two of her guests – Nigel Evans and Paul Morris – to cook their own main course.

TWO
Karen Bretagne pinned her hopes of winning on her pavlova. And she was determined to get it right. So when her first go didn't go to plan, she embarked on a second. Then a third. Then a fourth. And even a fifth. But none of them quite worked. So she had to cobble together the best bits – or perhaps we should say the least worst bits – cover them with cream and fruit, then keep her fingers crossed. But not even that could disguise the cock-up.

THREE
Christmas *Come Dine With Me*: Maria Greenhough came to make her chocolate and lemon pots, only to discover she didn't have enough eggs … because her husband had cooked them for breakfast that morning. So with the shops long since shut, she had to beg a couple from somewhere. Luckily one of her neighbours had some spare. And she went on to win the competition.

FOUR
In Liverpool, Terry White hoped to amaze his guests with some crêpes Suzette. The diners were amazed all right, but not by the quality of the pancakes – rather their strange blue colour. Terry had planned to flambé them with liqueur. But he hadn't realized that he'd picked up a blue-tinted version – and neither did he notice when he poured it over the pancakes. It certainly didn't help his chances, as he ended up way off the top of the table.

FIVE
Don't forget the vegetarian. And don't forget it's not just meat they don't like – but food that's cooked with meat. A mistake that Ernest Lehmenheim made when he entertained in Swansea. He wanted to serve cockles, bacon and laver bread – with a meat-free option without bacon for non-meat-eater Sue. But he still cooked her cockles in the bacon fat – and served it up to Sue. Luckily she asked him first – and he was forced to take the cockles back.

SIX
Cooking things in advance and reheating them. A time-honoured short-cut. But one that doesn't always deliver quite what you

expect. Marie Hughes-Price from Coventry cooked up smoked haddock fish cakes, topped with poached egg and hollandaise sauce. Determined to have as much done as possible beforehand, she cooked her eggs, then left them in ice-cold water, before reheating. She claims it always works; but James Paley may not have been so sure, as he had to leave the table whilst eating the eggs to be sick. But maybe he choked on something. Who can say.

SEVEN

You've served up a delicious starter and main – or so you think. Now all you need to round off the night is a delectable dessert and the prize could be yours. Then you go to serve up the pud, only to discover one of your guests is head down on the table, fast asleep. Or curled up on the sofa enjoying forty winks. It's happened: not once, not twice, but three times. Ask James Dean from Bournemouth, who wondered how he'd serve his chocolate pudding to Claudette when he saw her snoozing in his kitchen-diner. Or Jon Bramley, after guest Vera nodded off in his dining room. At least they woke to enjoy their dessert and give a final score. Spare a thought for Ronnie Masters, who had to deal with a guest, Chyna, who was so out for the count that she had to score the rest of the dinner the next day. Although it didn't seem

to make much difference – as Ronnie walked off with the prize.

EIGHT

Spend a bit of money on your ingredients – not just the booze – and don't go for anything too bizarre. Care-home owner Forbes Robertson decided to spend just 90p on pig's trotters for his main course – and his guests were distinctly unimpressed. Forbes tried to make up for it by washing the meat down with some quality champagne …

NINE

Don't leave your guests out on the doorstep. Even if they've arrived early, and you're busy in the kitchen, it's simply rude to not welcome them in. When one of her guests arrived early, Pippa Hudson from Leeds decided to leave her in the cold until preparations were done. Pippa paid the price when she came third.

TEN

And then there's the ultimate problem – the disappearing guest. Bernard Dorsett thought his dinner party was going great guns. Until one of his diners, Dawn, sloped off to bed before he served dessert. There wasn't even much consolation that the remaining guests enjoyed it: they found the poached pear rock hard. And the next day Dawn was equally dismissive about Mr Dorsett's dessert.

ten strange celebrity moments

Come Dine With Me isn't just about ordinary people – a whole host of celebrities, from pop star Lee Ryan of boyband Blue to TV presenter Linda Barker, have also taken up the challenge. Along the way they have dished up a mixture of fine food and culinary cock-ups, interspersed with some bizarre ideas of what will make for the perfect dinner party. Here is a selection of memorable moments.

ONE
Peter Stringfellow: the night-club impresario already had a tough job on his hands after his guests were less than impressed by his starter of tuna with olive oil ice cream. But things took a decided turn for the worse when his kitchen sink collapsed just before he came to dish up his main … With nowhere to drain his pans, he still managed to improvise and serve up his spaghetti …

TWO
Peter Stringfellow again. Undaunted by his disappearing sink, Peter ploughed on with

his main and dessert. Only for Michelle Heaton to find a long grey hair in her dessert. Suffice to say, there were no pets at the party.

THREE
Lesley Joseph, the actress best known for her role in *Birds of a Feather*, suffered any chef's ultimate nightmare: meat that wouldn't cook. Her slow-cooked lamb main course was so slow in cooking that guest Linda Lusardi suggested they should have dessert first. At one point all her guests were in the kitchen trying to help her prepare at least some meat that could be cooked and served.

FOUR
Anneka Rice: the broadcaster decided to cook a main course of paella and, because she'd never made it before, she borrowed a recipe off a friend. The only problem: when she came to cook the dish, she couldn't find her recipe. Anywhere. So she had to make it up as she went along. And in the ensuing panic, she managed to cut her finger.

FIVE

Lynsey de Paul: the singer and songwriter needed to make a dressing for her asparagus salad starter. But first she put too much lemon in. Then, when she tried again, she almost used vinegar that was four years out of date. Luckily for her diners, she read the label just in time.

SIX

Jonathan Ansell: the *X Factor* star and hit opera singer wanted to make some caramelized sugar for his dessert. But first he burnt the sugar. Then when he tried to cook off the burnt bits, he burnt it even more and managed to set off his fire alarm. Just as his first guest, Lynsey de Paul, arrived.

SEVEN

Jonathan Ansell again – this time joined by MC Harvey: Jonathan committed the ultimate table-setting faux pas by forgetting the cutlery for his starter. The problem seemed to be catching, as at the end of the competition Harvey also didn't put enough spoons on the table for his dessert.

EIGHT

Toby Young: the author decided to check whether his potatoes were cooked by feeding them to one of his children – only to see the spuds spat out. But his celebrity diners were

a bit less discerning and voted him the best host that week.

NINE

Caprice thought that the way to dinner party glory was to have dessert next to the swimming pool in her basement. But not before two synchronized swimmers performed in the water. Oddly enough, it wasn't quite enough to clinch her victory.

TEN

Nor was Jimmy Osmond's rather strange choice of assistant. He wanted a little help: so he hired someone who was just that: the diminutive Alan Bennett who's barely three foot tall. Then, to cap it all, he asked Alan to dress up as Elvis to introduce the dessert. His normally talkative celebrity guests were left rather dumb-founded. Funnily enough, Jimmy didn't win either.

starters

Benito Gundin

latkes & grilled vegetables with goat's cheese & basil oil

olive oil for greasing
4 medium-sized potatoes
1 large onion
2 tbsp chopped mixed fresh herbs (such
    as parsley, chives and tarragon)
1 organic free-range egg, beaten
1 tbsp white flour
1 aubergine, cut into 4 slices about 1cm thick
1 large or 2 medium courgettes, sliced into
    long strips
1 large red pepper, cored and cut into 8 long
    strips
4–5 tbsp virgin olive oil (I use Spanish: it's
    the best)
juice of 1 lemon
100g goat's cheese (Golden Cross is one of my
    favourites), cut into 4 slices about 1cm thick
basil oil and poudre de tomate (tomato powder),
    for garnish (optional)

Colour is very important in my cooking, and I chose the grilled vegetables because they look so good on the plate, although the preparation is a bit time-consuming. For the latkes I use Maris Piper potatoes – my friend Steven, who is a chef, says they are the best and I believe him.

1 Preheat the oven to 200°C/Gas 6. Grease 2 non-stick baking trays with olive oil.

2 To make the latkes, grate the potatoes and onion separately. Squeeze as much water out of the potatoes as you can, using your hands. Mix the onion and potato together and season generously with salt and freshly ground black pepper. Stir in the mixed herbs, beaten egg and flour. Divide the mixture into 4, then form each into a cake and place on one of the oiled baking trays.

3 Brush all the vegetables with the olive oil, season them and place on the other oiled tray.

4 Place both trays in the oven. Cook the latkes for 15–20 minutes until the underside is light brown, then pour a few drops of olive oil on top, turn them over and cook until light brown on the other side. Cook the vegetables until softened but not browned, which should take about the same amount of time as the latkes: 30–35 minutes. Take the trays from the oven. Keep the latkes somewhere warm. Put the vegetables in a bowl and sprinkle with lemon juice. You can prepare to this point ahead of time.

5 When ready to serve, preheat the grill to its hottest setting. Arrange the slices of aubergine on top of the latkes, then put the strips of courgette and red pepper on top. Place under the hot grill for about 5 minutes or until the vegetables are golden brown on the edges and the latkes are warmed through. Then place a slice of goat's cheese on each vegetable-topped latke and return to the heat for about 2 minutes or until the cheese starts to melt.

6 Transfer the latkes to warmed plates, garnish with the tomato powder and basil oil, if using, and serve.

Jane Bates

lock, stock & smokin' salmon, aka Vinny Jones

150g smoked salmon
2 tbsp double cream
220g cream cheese
a squeeze of lemon
pinch of dill weed
half a red chilli, finely chopped

TO SERVE
rocket leaves
olive oil, to drizzle
slices of lemon
1 baguette, sliced and crisped
   in the oven or toaster

SERVES FIVE

This was the starter for my Hollywood theme night. It's a straightforward salmon mousse, but with a twist – fresh chilli to give it an extra kick. I knew I'd got it right when one of the guests said he didn't like salmon mousse … before proceeding to scoff the lot! Delicious, if I say so myself.

1 Cut a few strips of smoked salmon for garnish, then put the rest into a blender along with the double cream, cream cheese, lemon juice, dill weed and chilli, and blend until smooth. Taste and season. Transfer to ramekins or other small dishes (125–150ml capacity), garnish with the strips of smoked salmon and put into the fridge to set.

2 Serve with rocket leaves drizzled with olive oil, a slice of lemon and crisped bread on the side.

Rebecca Hambley

mixed mezze

YOGHURT, CUCUMBER AND MINT DIP
500ml Greek yoghurt
1 clove garlic, crushed
½ medium cucumber, peeled and very
    finely diced
handful each of fresh mint and parsley,
    leaves finely chopped
½ tsp each ground cumin and coriander

CHICKPEA AND POMEGRANATE DIP
400g tin chickpeas
1 clove garlic, roasted in its skin
2 tbsp light tahini
2 tbsp lemon juice
½ tsp each cayenne pepper, ground
    coriander and cinnamon
the seeds of ½ pomegranate
1 tbsp pomegranate molasses
a little extra virgin olive oil and cayenne
    pepper, to serve

BROAD BEAN DIP
400g broad beans (frozen and thawed or fresh)
4 tbsp lemon juice
2 tbsp tahini
1 clove garlic, crushed
1 tsp ground coriander
leaves from a handful of fresh mint
extra virgin olive oil
handful of fresh parsley, leaves finely chopped

SERVES FOUR

This is a great way to start a dinner party. Not only do the mezze look spectacular, with such a range of colours and textures, but this is also a great ice-breaker. The sharing aspect automatically makes people relax in each other's company. Your guests might not have tried all these dishes before, so they quickly get chatting as they compare notes. Don't leave preparation until the last minute as it's quite time-consuming. They're good in the fridge for a couple of days so best to prepare them in advance, but make sure to serve them at room temperature.

Yoghurt, cucumber and mint dip
Mix the ingredients together and chill until required.

Chickpea and pomegranate dip
Drain the chickpeas, reserving the liquid. Squeeze the garlic from its skin. Put the chickpeas, garlic, tahini, lemon juice and spices into the blender or processor, along with as much of the reserved liquid as you need, and whiz to form a smooth paste. Transfer to a bowl and chill until required. When ready to serve, sprinkle the pomegranate seeds over the dip and drizzle with the pomegranate molasses and a little olive oil and extra cayenne pepper.

Broad bean dip
Briefly boil the broad beans, then cool and peel off the outer shell to reveal the bright green kernel. Whiz the beans, lemon juice, tahini, garlic, coriander and mint in a blender or processor, slowly adding olive oil until you have a smooth paste (keep it chunky if you prefer). Chill until required and sprinkle with fresh parsley just before serving.

MARINATED RED PEPPERS AND COURGETTES
2–3 red peppers
2–3 courgettes
lemon juice and extra virgin olive oil
fresh coriander, finely chopped, to serve

Marinated red peppers and courgettes

Roast the red peppers whole in a hot oven for about 30 minutes. Remove them from the oven, place in a paper bag and crunch up to seal, so that the peppers steam. After 10 minutes the skins of the red peppers can be peeled off easily. Meanwhile, thickly slice the courgettes, brush with oil and cook over a high heat in a griddle pan for about 3 minutes each side. Arrange on a plate and drizzle with lots of lemon juice and extra virgin olive oil. Remove the skins and seeds of the peppers, slice into quarters and add to the courgettes. Again, drizzle with lots of lemon juice and olive oil. Chill until required and sprinkle with fresh coriander just before serving.

Marinated olives

Get some good quality deli olives, drizzle with lemon juice and extra virgin olive oil and sprinkle with fresh parsley and mint.

Dan Churchill

chilled melon with parma ham, parmesan cheese & rocket

1 honeydew melon, chilled
2 handfuls rocket leaves
5 tbsp extra virgin olive oil
2 tbsp balsamic vinegar
5 mint leaves, chopped
10–12 strips Parma ham
10–12 shavings Parmesan cheese

I lived in Italy for three wonderful years and became a huge fan of Parma ham. It's beautiful and can be dressed in all sorts of ways, but never better than with melon – the classic bitter-sweet combination. It's nice and light like a glass of champagne, perfect for freshening the taste buds for the feast to come. But the fruit must be cold, as there's nothing worse than lukewarm melon. This is quick and easy to knock together, perfect for a busy dinner party.

1 Cut the honeydew melon into 5 or 6 wedges and remove the seeds. Place each wedge of melon on a serving plate and arrange the rocket leaves around and over the fruit.

2 Arrange Parmesan shavings and 2 strips of Parma ham over each wedge of melon.

3 Whisk the oil and vinegar together in a small bowl. Stir the mint in, grind a little black pepper over, then pour a little around each plate and over the rocket leaves and serve.

Daniel Fletcher

terrine of spring onion & chicken in parma ham

300g Parma ham, thinly sliced (about
    18 slices, but you might not need it all)
110g self-raising flour
3 eggs
2 tbsp milk
2 cooked chicken breasts, in small chunks
100g Gruyère cheese, grated
2 bunches of spring onions, trimmed but
    kept whole

TO SERVE
rocket and basil leaves
3 heaped tbsp cranberry sauce
2 tbsp balsamic vinegar
1 tbsp extra virgin olive oil

SERVES FOUR TO SIX

This terrine is the ultimate family dish, passed down from generation to generation, with each new generation adding their own twist. In my case, it's to wrap the terrine in Parma ham. I like my starters to be intricate and full of flavour — and this ticks those boxes — and, crucially, I wanted to use quite 'accessible' meats. I didn't want to run the risk of losing points just because someone didn't like the taste of, say, venison or offal!

1 Preheat the oven to 180°C/Gas 4. Line a 1kg loaf tin with the Parma ham, leaving the ends hanging over.

2 Put the flour into a bowl, break in the eggs and whisk until well combined, then add the milk and whisk some more. Add the chicken and Gruyère and stir well.

3 Spoon half the mixture into the lined tin, then put in a layer of the spring onions running lengthways. Add the rest of the terrine mixture to the tin and fold over the excess ham to enclose the filling. Place the terrine in a roasting dish. Pour boiling water into the dish to come about halfway up the sides of the terrine, to make a bain-marie. Cover the terrine with foil and bake in the bain-marie for 1 hour, removing the foil for the last 10 minutes.

4 Leave to cool, then set aside in the fridge to firm up. Remove from the fridge before serving and give it enough time to return to room temperature. Turn out and cut into slices — with a serrated knife is easiest.

5 Serve each person with a slice of terrine on a bed of rocket and basil. Whisk together the cranberry, balsamic vinegar and olive oil and serve alongside, for your guests to help themselves, or drizzled over the plates — as you prefer.

Matthew Baxter

tortelloni, mozzarella & tomato in basil leaf

1 pack of tortelloni – spinach and
    ricotta is best
30 bocconcini (little mozzarella balls)
30 sun-blushed tomatoes (or 15 halved,
    if large)
30 large basil leaves
30 cocktail sticks
cracked black pepper

SERVES SIX TO TEN

I'm told that tortelloni was my favourite food even at
the age of four, and this has now become my signature
dish. I adapted it from an old recipe of my aunt Lucy,
and these days I always make it for our family Christmas
party. I love the way it looks – it obeys the old Italian
'tricolore' principle. This is a great canapé.

1 Bring a large pan of water to the boil, add large-grain salt
and a touch of olive oil, then cook the tortelloni for a few
minutes, according to the packet instructions. Drain and
set aside to cool thoroughly. Take a piece of pasta, place
a bocconcino on top and a sun-blushed tomato on top
of that, and wrap in a basil leaf. Spear with a cocktail stick
to hold it together. Arrange 3 or 5 to a plate (food should
never be served in even numbers …), dust with cracked
black pepper and serve.

Ronnie Masters

asparagus salad with lemon & shallot dressing

16–20 asparagus spears, woody ends
    trimmed
2 large handfuls of mixed leaves (I like
    to include curly endive among them)
200g feta cheese
4 small vine tomatoes, halved, deseeded
    and sliced

FOR THE DRESSING
1 tsp Dijon mustard
2 tbsp lemon juice
2 shallots, very finely chopped
6–7 tbsp mild olive oil

SERVES FOUR

This is an excellent option as a starter when serving a heavier main course. The flavours of the lemon, feta and asparagus are superb together. As the dressing can be prepared in advance, this is a winner for a quick, easy and flavoursome dish. Make sure to serve the asparagus with a bit of bite; steaming it is the best way. Serve with warm crusty bread.

1 Steam the asparagus for 3–5 minutes until tender at the tip but still with a little bite in the stalk. Set aside to cool down.

2 To make the dressing, combine the mustard, lemon juice and shallots in a bowl. Slowly whisk in the olive oil, ensuring the dressing does not become too thick or too oily. Season with black pepper.

3 Arrange a handful of mixed leaves on each plate, then place 4–5 asparagus spears in a fan on top. Crumble the feta cheese over the leaves and place the tomato around the side for colour. Drizzle with a little dressing, and serve.

Nick Cooper

pork terrine

1.2kg lean and fat pork from belly and
   shoulder, minced or finely chopped
200g pig's liver, minced or finely chopped
seasonings to taste: salt, pepper, thyme,
   garlic, allspice, nutmeg, mace, sage
rashers of streaky bacon to line the dish
tiny pickled onions, to serve

Often regarded as the preserve of professional chefs,
a terrine is really a traditional staple of the farmhouse
kitchen. What makes them so good is the almost endless
variety of ingredients you can use: different meats and
different cuts, different alcohols and different spices.
It's the constant basting from the fat during the slow
cooking that makes the dish. This is ideal prepare-ahead
dinner-party food, delicious with home-made chutney.

1 Combine the meat and liver, season to taste and leave
for 24 hours.

2 Preheat the oven to 120°C/Gas ½. Line a large terrine or
loaf tin with the bacon, letting some overhang if necessary,
then fill with the meat and liver mix, pressing gently to
exclude any air pockets, and fold the excess bacon over
the top. Cover the top with foil, and place the terrine in
a roasting dish. Pour boiling water into the dish to come
about halfway up the sides of the terrine, to make a bain-
marie. Cook the terrine in the bain-marie for 2 hours, or
until the meat appears to float in its fat. Pierce the centre
with a skewer: the juices should run clear. Take the terrine
out of the bain-marie, remove the foil and allow to cool.
Then cover with fresh foil, put a weight on top and put
it in the fridge to press for 24 hours.

3 Turn out, slice and serve.

Juliet Harbutt

arbroath smokies pâté with roasted red peppers & red onions

1 pair Arbroath smokies
zest and juice of ½ lemon
pinch of cayenne pepper
225g cream cheese
150ml double cream

FOR THE ROASTED PEPPERS
oil for roasting
2 red peppers, cut in half lengthways
    and deseeded
2 red onions, quartered lengthways
225g tinned tomatoes
a little fresh thyme

TO SERVE
hot, chunky toast fingers

SERVES SIX

Arbroath smokies are a speciality of the small town of the same name on the east coast of Scotland. Locally caught haddock, smoked over hardwood until it shines like bronze, the smokie is an absolute treat, now made by less than a handful of producers but protected under the PDO scheme (Protected Designation of Origin). Taking the bones out is a pain but when mixed with the cream cheese and lemon it melts on warm toast and tastes like heaven – unless, of course, like one of my guests, you don't like fish!

1 Flake the flesh of the smokies with a fork, leaving any skin and bones behind. Transfer to a food processor along with the lemon zest and juice and cayenne pepper and whiz until well blended but not too smooth. Add the cream cheese and whiz, then the double cream. Don't overblend – you don't want the mixture to be too processed. Season with salt and freshly ground black pepper, then spoon into 6 individual ramekins, cover with foil and chill for 2 hours or overnight.

2 For the red peppers, preheat the oven to 180°C/Gas 4 and lightly oil a roasting dish. Put the peppers in the dish, cut-side up, and put a quarter of red onion inside each one, with the remainder in the dish. Divide the tinned tomatoes equally between the peppers. Drizzle with oil, sprinkle with 2 tbsp water, season to taste with salt, pepper and fresh thyme, then bake for 45 minutes or until soft. Allow to cool slightly, then slice. Serve warm or cold, alongside the pâté, with hot toast fingers.

Nicky Clarke

spaghetti vongole

450g spaghetti
4 tbsp extra-virgin olive oil, plus extra to serve
3 cloves garlic, chopped or crushed
1–2 red chillies, chopped (seeds included
    according to taste)
small bunch of fresh parsley, finely chopped
1kg small clams, scrubbed and de-gritted

SERVES FOUR

My mother is Greek, so I grew up immersed in Mediterranean cuisine and I have been drawn to these kinds of flavours ever since. This particular dish is easy to throw together, and works equally well as a main. Personally I always use fresh clams, but if these are hard to come by there's no reason why you couldn't use tinned or preserved clams. As for the chilli, use as much or as little as your palate can stand. Just don't do what I did, and make the schoolboy error of rubbing your eyes while chopping!

1 Cook the pasta in a large pan of boiling, salted water according to the instructions on the packet.

2 In another pan, heat the olive oil and gently sauté the garlic, chilli and half the parsley on a low heat for a few minutes. Add the clams and turn up the heat, then cover and steam for 4–5 minutes, or until the clams have opened. Discard any clams that remain closed.

3 Remove about a third of the clams from their shells. Drain the spaghetti and transfer to a large, warmed bowl. Toss the clams, with and without shells, and all the juices and flavourings from the pan with the spaghetti. Sprinkle over the remaining parsley. Add a little more olive oil and season to taste, then toss again before serving.

Seamus Farrelly

scallops in angel-hair pasta

400g fine angel-hair pasta
16–24 king or queen scallops,
    washed and trimmed
120g unsalted butter
3 tbsp fresh lime juice
2 tbsp chopped tarragon

I love seared scallops. Fresh lime juice, for me, adds that cutting edge, enhancing the subtle touch of anise that comes from the fresh tarragon. Simple from pan to plate.

1 Cook the pasta in a large pot of boiling, salted water until al dente (according to the instructions on the packet).

2 Pat the scallops dry and season with salt and pepper. Heat half the butter in a large non-stick frying pan over moderate heat until the foam subsides, then sauté half the scallops, turning, until golden: 2–3 minutes. Transfer with a slotted spoon to a bowl. Add the rest of the butter to the pan and cook the remaining scallops in the same way. Return the first batch of scallops to the pan and stir in the lime juice and tarragon.

3 Keeping 3–4 tbsp of the pasta-cooking water, drain the pasta. Toss the pasta in a warmed bowl with half the scallops and the reserved cooking water. Top with the remaining scallops and sauce, check the seasoning and serve at once.

Stephen Mahon

portobello mushrooms with gruyère & red leicester

50g butter, plus extra for greasing
6 large flat mushrooms, cleaned
3 red onions, finely chopped
pinch of fresh marjoram or dried oregano
100g red Leicester, grated
50g Gruyère, grated
100ml double cream

This looks like you've gone to a lot of trouble, but actually it's dead simple. I chose Gruyère and red Leicester because they grill well, and they've got good earthy flavours that complement the mushrooms. Go for a mammoth mushroom – the bigger the better – and don't skimp on the double cream. This is no dieter's delight, it's strictly for foodies.

1 Lightly butter a baking tray. Trim and discard the tip of the mushroom stalks and place the caps upside down on the tray. Season with salt and pepper. Using half the butter, put a small piece on each of the mushrooms.

2 Melt the remaining butter in a large pan over a medium-high heat and, once sizzling, add the onions. Fry for 8–10 minutes until softened and lightly coloured. Add the herbs and season to taste.

3 Meanwhile, preheat the grill to hot and cook the mushrooms for 6–8 minutes or until tender. Mix the two cheeses in a bowl, stir in the cream and set aside until the mushrooms and onions are done.

4 Spoon the onions on top of the mushrooms, then top with the cheese mixture. Return to the grill until the cheese has melted to a golden brown. Serve at once.

Steve Parks

minted pea cappuccino with porcini dust, truffle oil & parmesan wafers

10g dried porcini
100g Parmesan cheese, grated
25g unsalted butter
1 small onion, finely chopped
1 clove garlic, finely chopped
a good handful of mint, chopped
450g peas, fresh podded or frozen
    and thawed
500ml light vegetable stock
125ml semi-skimmed milk
truffle oil, for drizzling

SERVES FOUR

I came up with this specially for the show, because I wanted to make an impact. Each of the ingredients mirrors those of a normal cappuccino: porcini dust for the chocolate on top, Parmesan wafers for the sweet biscuits on the side, and the whole thing frothed up using the steam jet on my coffee maker. Fun and delicious, because first impressions count!

1 Grind the porcini to a fine powder in a coffee grinder and set aside.

2 Spread the grated Parmesan cheese over a non-stick pan, heat until melted and golden, then remove the disc from the pan and cut it into wafers.

3 Heat the butter in a medium-sized saucepan over a moderate heat, add the onion, garlic and mint and cook gently until soft. Add the peas and stir to coat in the buttery onions. Pour in the stock, bring to a simmer and cook until the peas are soft. Season to taste with salt, freshly ground black pepper and a pinch of sugar. Whiz in a blender until smooth. Pour through a sieve into a clean saucepan, reheat and check seasoning.

4 Pour the soup into warm mugs, reserving 1 tbsp for foaming. Pour the milk and the reserved soup into a jug and foam using the nozzle on a coffee machine. Spoon the foam over the soup. Sprinkle with porcini dust and drizzle with truffle oil. Serve with Parmesan wafers on the side.

Toby Young

tomato tarts

1 packet ready-made puff pastry
Dijon mustard
5 large good quality tomatoes
150g Gruyère cheese, grated
1 egg, beaten

My starter was something I'd never cooked before but my wife has made many, many times. With her advice, it proved relatively easy – and went down very well. It can be prepared in advance then put into the oven at the last minute and served with a flourish as a warm starter.

1 Preheat the oven to 180°C/Gas 4.

2 Roll out the ready-made puff pastry to a thickness of about 5mm. Cut out 5 discs of about 15cm (check the size of the plate you will be serving them on). Make an indentation with a slightly smaller circular object, e.g. a glass, so that you end up with a circle within a circle, with about 1cm between the two.

3 Place the 5 pastry discs on a baking sheet. Spread Dijon mustard over the inner circle. Slice the tomatoes and layer the slices on top of the mustard. Sprinkle the tomatoes with a pinch of sugar, salt and pepper. Put the grated cheese on top. With a brush or a finger, paint the outer circle with beaten egg to glaze it.

4 Bake for 20–25 minutes until the pastry is golden brown and well risen. Serve warm.

Jim Blythe

pork satay with courgette salad

1kg pork, cut into bite-size pieces
3 tbsp peanut butter
1 tbsp soy sauce
chilli powder, to taste

FOR THE SALAD
1 large courgette
1 red chilli, seeded and finely chopped
2 tbsp lime juice
1 tbsp sugar

SERVES SIX

Satay is a classic Indonesian or Malaysian sauce, and although pork is not typical – Indonesia and Malaysia are both mainly Muslim countries – the meat actually goes wonderfully well with the sauce. The courgette salad is Thai, and my daughter showed me how to make it when she got back from Thailand. It tastes good and is very clean in the mouth, a perfect foil for the pork and peanuts. You'll need satay sticks or metal skewers for this.

1 Thread the pork pieces onto 12 or 18 satay sticks or metal skewers (depending on size). Put the peanut butter, soy sauce and chilli powder with a roughly equal amount of water into a bowl and briefly microwave it: beware, it tends to boil over! Check the consistency regularly and add more water as necessary – the peanut butter absorbs a lot. Aim for a sauce with a consistency like that of thick hot chocolate.

2 Meanwhile, preheat the grill to medium-hot. Grill the pork, turning so that it's evenly coloured on all sides and cooked right through: 12–15 minutes.

3 Just before the pork is ready, grate the raw courgette and mix it with the chillies, lime juice and sugar. The courgette tends to lose water fast, so it can't be prepared in advance. When the pork is ready, arrange the skewers on individual plates and pour the satay sauce over them. Pile the courgette salad alongside and serve immediately. You could also serve the satay on one large serving plate, with the salad in another dish, for guests to help themselves.

Ian Cook

roasted butternut squash & red lentil soup with pesto oil & garlic croutons

1 small butternut squash, cut into chunks
1 medium onion, finely chopped
1 red pepper, finely chopped
1 carrot, finely chopped
1 potato, chopped
1 clove garlic
olive oil, for frying
450ml vegetable stock
100g split red lentils
1 bay leaf

FOR THE GARLIC CROUTONS
5 thick slices wholemeal bread,
    crusts removed, cut into cubes
1 clove garlic, finely chopped

FOR THE PESTO OIL
1 tbsp good quality pesto sauce
4 tbsp extra virgin olive oil (the best
    you can get)

SERVES FIVE

To be honest, all I wanted to do was not make a prat of myself and to get on with the other four people. I composed my menu after many, many hours of discussion and thought. In the end two-thirds of my menu was vegan, for Nicky, my vegan guest. But I didn't call my soup a 'vegan soup'. It's just a good soup, and I didn't want Nicky to feel singled out or the others to feel they were getting anything strange!

1 Roast the butternut squash in a hot oven (200°C/Gas 6) for 20 minutes. (The peel on a small squash will be fine enough to cook and eat.)

2 Sweat all the remaining vegetables and garlic in a good glug of olive oil in a large saucepan until slightly translucent. Add the roasted squash, stock, lentils and bay leaf, and season to taste. Simmer for 30 minutes, then allow to cool and purée in a blender (after removing the bay leaf).

3 Fry the bread cubes in a good glug of olive oil with the garlic until just golden brown. Set aside.

4 Mix the pesto and the olive oil together well.

5 Return the soup to the pan and reheat gently before serving, adjusting the consistency with a little extra water if needed or stock. Serve with a drizzle of pesto oil on top and the garlic croutons alongside.

Darren Frame

slow-cooked chilli with nachos

1 tbsp olive oil
1 large onion, finely diced
2 cloves garlic, chopped
400g good quality beef mince
1 tbsp chilli powder, or more to taste
splash of Worcestershire sauce
splash of soy sauce
big splash of Tabasco sauce
400g tin kidney beans in chilli sauce
400g tin chopped tomatoes
4 tbsp tomato purée, or more to taste
nachos (off the shelf)

SERVES FOUR TO SIX

I love rich and spicy food. I use my slow cooker for this, preparing the chilli in the morning and then letting it slow-cook all day, which gives the flavours plenty of time to mix and mature. I like my guests to be wowed by a rich flavour on the tongue rather than a huge portion on the plate. Nachos make the perfect dipping tool.

1 Heat the olive oil in a large frying pan over moderate heat and fry the onion and garlic until translucent but not browned. Add the mince and stir until it has just coloured all over. Sprinkle the chilli powder over and stir well. Splash with Worcestershire sauce, soy sauce and Tabasco sauce (to taste, but be generous).

2 Pour in the beans and their sauce, the chopped tomatoes and tomato purée and heat through until simmering. Season, then taste and adjust the flavourings before transferring to a slow cooker. Cook on low for 5–6 hours, or until ready to serve, checking and stirring regularly. If the consistency becomes very thick, thin with a little water.

3 Serve in a big bowl with lots of nachos for dipping.

Simone Burns

fisherman's surprise

1 large live crab, kept in the freezer
5 rustic bread rolls, plus 1–2 spares
olive oil, for frying
3 sticks celery with leaves, roughly
    chopped
1 large onion, roughly chopped
1 carrot, roughly chopped
125ml white wine
juice of 1 lemon

SERVES FIVE

When I was nineteen, on holiday with my first love, we hitchhiked down La Nueva Carretera from the US to Mexico. On a white sandy beach on the Gulf of California, we came across a quaint waterfront restaurant, which served us this wonderful soup in bread-roll 'bowls'. I have spent years trying to replicate the dish – and I think I have finally succeeded.

1 First, prepare the bread rolls. Cut off the tops; these will be the 'lids'. Remove the soft centres, being careful not to make any holes, and reserve. Place the empty rolls and their lids on a baking tray and set aside.

2 Heat some olive oil in a stockpot, add the vegetables and briefly sauté them. Then add the wine and 500ml water. Bring to the boil, then drop in the crab (straight from the freezer) and cook it for 15–20 minutes.

3 Remove the crab and leave to cool. Drain the stock and set aside. Once the crab is cool, remove the meat from the claws. Dice the meat, cover and put aside.

4 Heat some oil in a large saucepan, add the empty claw pieces and feet (not the body) and stir-fry for 2 minutes, then add the drained stock. Bring to a simmer and cook very gently for 30 minutes. Drain again, return the stock to the pan and add the bread roll inners. Blend the soup using a hand-held blender – be careful, because the soup is hot. If the soup is not thick enough, use some of the spare white bread to thicken it some more. Add the crab meat and heat through. Do not allow the soup to boil again but keep it simmering over moderate heat. Season to taste with salt, pepper and lemon juice.

5 Meanwhile, preheat the oven to 200°C/Gas 6. Heat the bread rolls for 3 minutes. Then arrange them on suitable plates, fill up with soup, being careful not to spill any, nor to fill them too full, place the lids on and serve.

Linda Barker

cauliflower soup with goat's cheese & truffle oil & home-made rolls

50g butter
150g white onion, finely chopped
250g leeks, finely sliced
200g cauliflower, in florets
900ml chicken stock, boiling
100ml double cream
50g strong(ish) goat's cheese, pushed
    through a sieve
truffle oil and snipped chives, to serve

FOR THE BREAD ROLLS
225g plain flour
225g wholemeal flour
1 packet fast-action yeast (1½ tsp)
1 tsp caster sugar
2 tsp salt
2 tbsp oil
290ml warm water
oil to grease
6 tbsp mixed seeds
1 egg, beaten, for glazing

SERVES FOUR

This is actually a very easy soup, but brings a touch of glamour to a dinner party with the addition of the goat's cheese and truffle oil. Just two small ingredients to turn a one-star dish into five-star luxury!

1 First make the bread rolls. Sift the flours into a bowl, then add the yeast and sugar and stir well. Add the salt, oil and water, combine well using your hands until you have a dough, then knead for 10 minutes. Place the dough in a separate, oiled bowl, cover with clingfilm and leave to rise in a warm place for an hour.

2 Knock the dough back then sprinkle in most of the seeds. Knead again for 10 minutes. Separate into about 12 pieces and form them into rolls. Leave to rise for about 1 hour.

3 Preheat the oven to 200°C/Gas 6. Glaze the tops of the rolls with beaten egg and sprinkle with the remaining seeds. Bake for about 20 minutes until golden.

4 For the soup, melt the butter in a saucepan, add the onions and leeks, stir well, then cover and cook gently for 8–10 minutes without letting them colour. Add the cauliflower, stir well and sweat for another 5 minutes. Meanwhile, bring the stock to the boil, then pour it into the pan and simmer the soup for 10–15 minutes until the cauliflower is soft.

5 Allow to cool slightly, then blend in the saucepan using a hand-held blender (or transfer to a liquidizer). Then, just before serving, stir in the cream and goat's cheese and warm through for 5 minutes. Pour into warmed soup bowls, drizzle with truffle oil and sprinkle with chives. Serve the bread on the side.

James Paley

crab & red pepper soup

2 live crabs
1 white onion
4 red peppers
knob of butter and 2 tbsp olive oil, for frying
5 cloves garlic, finely chopped
2 chicken stock cubes
sprinkling of fresh thyme leaves
150ml double cream
6 fresh basil leaves, chopped

I love the fact that this is so simple to prepare, but it still seems to pack a wow factor when you serve it up. Crab has a big, strong flavour and works really well with the herbs. The fresher the crab the better – personally, I always use live crabs. A lot of people find red pepper quite bland, but the secret is in the preparation: a little bit of pre-frying draws the flavours out.

1 Put the crabs in the freezer for 20 minutes to send them to sleep. While this is happening, trim and finely chop the onion and red peppers. Melt the butter in the olive oil in a large saucepan, add the onion and red pepper and cook until softened. Stir in the garlic and cook until the aroma is released. Then pour in 1.2 litres water and bring to the boil. Crumble in the stock cubes and add a good grinding of pepper and a sprinkling of thyme, and reduce the heat to a simmer.

2 Meanwhile, bring a large pot of water to the boil for the crabs. Add plenty of salt then drop in the drowsy crabs, reduce the heat slightly and cook for 20 minutes. Run the cooked crabs under cold water until thoroughly cold, then extract all the meat, remembering to discard the dead man's fingers. Don't forget the claws: there's lots of meat in them.

3 Add the crab meat to your saucepan and blend everything together with a hand blender, then simmer for 10 minutes. Finally, stir in the cream and add the basil leaves, taste and adjust the seasoning, and simmer for a few minutes until heated right through. Serve at once.

Carla Wisdom-Gray

'soul in a bowl': spicy sweetcorn soup

knob of butter and 2 tbsp olive oil,
    for cooking
1 small red onion, finely chopped
2 cloves garlic, finely chopped
2 sticks celery, finely chopped
1 red chilli, finely chopped
half yellow pepper, chopped
500ml vegetable stock
340g tin sweetcorn, drained and rinsed
400ml tin coconut milk

SERVES FOUR

This is easy, comforting food – homely and hearty, a real winter warmer with a lot of kick to it. It's simplicity itself to make. You can use whatever chillies you like, but I always go for Scotch bonnets – they pack a lot of heat, so be warned!

1 In a large saucepan, gently melt the butter in the oil, then add the onion, garlic, celery, chilli and yellow pepper and sweat until soft: 5–10 minutes. Add the vegetable stock and sweetcorn, bring to the boil, then reduce the heat and simmer for 5 minutes.

2 Purée the soup using a liquidizer or a hand-held blender (allow the soup to cool slightly first to avoid being splashed with hot soup), then stir in the coconut milk. Season to taste, and gently reheat to serve.

Main Courses

Ian Cook

fillet of tofu & chestnut with garlic potato cakes & spicy tomato sauce

FOR THE FILLETS OF TOFU
175g silken tofu
1 shallot, chopped
3 tbsp dry sage and onion stuffing mix
200g mushrooms, chopped
250g can chestnuts, drained
425g can butter beans, drained

FOR THE GARLIC POTATO CAKES
3 or 4 large potatoes, such as Maris Piper,
    boiled and cut into thick slices (you need 10)
2 tbsp finely chopped shallots
1 large clove garlic, very finely sliced
olive oil, for greasing and frying

FOR THE SPICY TOMATO SAUCE
2 shallots, finely chopped
1 small red chilli, finely chopped (with
    or without seeds according to taste)
1 clove garlic, crushed
1 tbsp olive oil
2 × 400g tins chopped tomatoes
splash of red wine
sugar, to taste

SERVES FIVE

I served two main courses. One was seabass in a classic Italian style, with lemon juice and olive oil, with potato cakes alongside. For Nicky, my vegan guest, I added this fillet of tofu to the menu and slightly adapted the potato cakes to these dairy-free, garlic-rich ones.

1 Preheat the oven to 200°C/Gas 6. Oil 2 baking sheets.

2 Place all the ingredients for the fillet of tofu in a food processor and briefly whiz to combine. Don't overblend: you want to maintain a bit of texture. Season with salt and plenty of freshly ground black pepper. Using metallic rings about 7cm across and 3.5cm deep, shape into 5 cakes. You need to press the contents in well so that they keep their shape when you remove the rings. Transfer the tofu fillets to one of the oiled baking sheets and bake for 30 minutes.

3 Meanwhile, reusing the metallic rings, wipe them clean then lightly oil the insides. Press in a layer of cooked potato, covering all the base. Add a fifth of the shallots and garlic. Add another layer of potato, smoothing out with the back of a spoon. Remove the ring, and continue until you've made 5 cakes. In a frying pan, gently brown one side of the potato cakes in a little oil: about 2 minutes. Transfer the potato cakes to the second oiled baking sheet, turning them over as you do so, so that the lightly browned side is uppermost, and add to the oven for the final 20 minutes of cooking.

4 To make the spicy tomato sauce, sweat the shallots with the chilli and garlic in the oil in a saucepan. Add the tomatoes and red wine, then cook over a gentle heat, stirring from time to time, until nicely reduced and thickened. Taste and season, adding a tiny amount of sugar to balance the sauce out. Purée and pass through a fine sieve. Reheat, if necessary, to serve.

Matthew Baxter

red mullet with potato, beans & tapenade

5 red mullets, filleted
500g waxy potatoes (Exquisa
    or Charlotte are great)
pinch of saffron strands
200g fine green beans
olive oil

FOR THE TAPENADE
10 anchovies
15 olives, pitted
2 cloves garlic

SERVES FIVE

Red mullet is what I call a real chef's fish. In fact, a lot of chefs will tell you it's their favourite. It has an oily texture and a very distinctive flavour, making it a bit more challenging than your average fish. It was a bit of a gamble serving it up on the night and it could have backfired horribly, but luckily my fellow diners seemed to approve. This proved to me that they were all proper chefs themselves!

1 You could ask your fishmonger to fillet the mullets. Check for and remove pin-bones.

2 For the tapenade, cut the anchovies, olives and garlic together using scissors, adding a bit of olive oil if too dry. Season well and leave in a ramekin.

3 Boil the waxy potatoes with a touch of saffron in the water, then drain. Liberally drizzle with olive oil and season well. Boil the beans with a good pinch of sea salt. Meanwhile, douse the fish in olive oil, salt and pepper and place under a very hot grill, turning only once. It will cook in a matter of moments. Serve on heated plates.

Benito Gundin

baked seabass with potatoes, fennel & tomato sauce

FOR THE FISH
1 wild seabass or royal sea bream
    or emperor, about 1.8kg
4 lemons: 2 for juice and 2 for slicing
1kg potatoes, thinly sliced
1 large onion, roughly chopped
1 large fennel, roughly chopped
4 large cloves garlic
pinch of saffron (use authentic Spanish
    saffron, the flavour is amazing)
70g parsley, chopped
5 tbsp Spanish extra virgin olive oil

FOR THE TOMATO SAUCE
3 tbsp extra virgin olive oil
1 clove garlic, crushed
1 small onion, finely chopped
½ green pepper, diced
½ courgette, diced
4 medium mushrooms, such as chestnut
    mushrooms, diced
bouquet of herbs, such as thyme, bay leaves,
    oregano and savory (found in good delis)
good splash of red wine
400g tin chopped tomatoes

SERVES FOUR

I'm from Spain, and I really wanted to include a Spanish dish on my menu. My mother makes this, Lubina al horno, every Christmas, but without the fennel, which isn't popular in Spain. So now that I've added fennel I can claim this recipe as my own! Instead of one large fish, you can also make this with four small bream or bass of about 500g each. Using wild seabass can be tricky, however, as they tend to hide in cupboards … The tomato sauce tastes much, much better made the day before.

1 First, prepare the tomato sauce (preferably a day ahead). Warm the olive oil over a gentle heat in a heavy-based saucepan, then add the garlic, onion and green pepper and cook until soft. Season generously. Add the courgette, mushrooms and bouquet of herbs, and cook until the mushrooms are softening. Add the red wine and cook for 8–10 minutes. Then pour in the tomatoes and simmer at very, very low heat for 45 minutes at least. Check the seasoning and add a pinch of sugar to balance the acidity. Continue simmering until it looks and tastes really good. Remove and discard the herbs.

2 Preheat the oven to 190°C/Gas 5. Take the fish and make 3 deep cuts to the bone on both sides across the thickest part. Season inside and out, making sure the salt and pepper gets inside the cuts. Place the fish in a large dish and pour lemon juice over it, rubbing it in well. Set the fish aside.

3 On a greased ovenproof dish, large enough to take the whole fish, arrange the potato, onion and fennel. In a large mortar, mash the garlic, saffron, a large pinch of salt and the parsley (leaving some for garnishing the dish later) with a pestle until you have a thick paste, then add 4 tbsp of the olive oil and 5 tbsp water and stir well. Spoon evenly over the potato, onion and fennel.

4 Bake the potato mixture in the oven for about 40 minutes, until almost cooked, then take it out. Insert ½ slice of lemon in each cut made previously in the fish and put the fish on top of the potatoes. Pour over the remaining tablespoon of olive oil and return to the oven for 25 minutes, until the fish is just cooked.

5 On a large round white plate, place the fish, and next to it the potatoes, onion and fennel. Into a small ramekin, pour the tomato sauce (reheated if made ahead). Garnish with the parsley and serve at once.

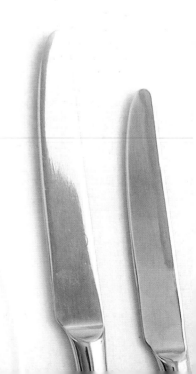

Bill Buckley

skate with roast asparagus, butter bean mash & lime & caper butter sauce

125g butter
2 large onions, finely chopped
4 cloves garlic, finely chopped
3 × 400g tins butter beans
4 tbsp double cream
handful of flat-leaf parsley
6 small skate wings (large ones
   can be cut in half to serve 2)
4 limes
splash of white wine
olive oil
36 medium-thick asparagus spears
small jar of capers, drained

Skate has long been my favourite fish and I love to cook it in many different ways. It's fabulous pan-fried, but that method is tricky when you're cooking for large numbers, so bunging it in the oven covered with foil and with some liquid to keep it moist seemed the best idea on the night. I can't remember how I came to invent the mash but it's really creamy, delicious and unusual, while the asparagus adds a touch of luxury. I was thrilled when Serena, an avowed fish-hater, cleaned her plate!

1 Melt 25g of the butter in a large pan. Very slowly cook the onions and garlic over the lowest possible heat until completely soft but not coloured: if your hob goes down low enough, this could take as long as an hour – the slower the better.

2 Drain the butter beans. Rinse them thoroughly and drain again. Put them into a food processor, season and add the cream. Tip in the onion/garlic 'sludge' with any remaining butter from the pan. Process until you have a smooth paste. You will probably have to do this in batches. You might want to push it all through a sieve to ensure silky smoothness, or you might prefer the odd 'rustic' lump. Set aside.

3 Preheat the oven to 180°C/Gas 4.

4 Cut the thick stalks off the parsley, reserving the leaves. Arrange the skate wings in a single layer in a baking tray or trays. Tuck in the parsley stalks. Cut one of the limes into 6 or 8 segments and tuck those around too. Splash a little wine over and season with a little salt and freshly ground black pepper. Cover with foil and bake for 15–20 minutes until the flesh is white all the way through.

5 Meanwhile, dribble a little olive oil into another baking tray. Cut the hard ends off the asparagus spears. Season. Tip the spears into the oiled tray and mix with your hands to get them coated in the oil. Bake in the same oven as the skate for about the same amount of time.

6 Tip the butter bean mash into a large pan and heat very slowly and gently until piping hot.

7 Grate the rind from 2 of the limes and squeeze the juice. Heat the remaining butter until it melts. Add half the rind and juice, and the capers, and taste. If it needs more sharpening up, add more rind and juice. Finely chop the reserved parsley leaves at the last possible moment and stir them in too.

8 Put a dollop of hot mash in the centre of each plate. Lay half a dozen asparagus spears across the top. Drain the skate wings briefly and balance one on top. (If the mash looks too thick, let it down slightly using the delicious liquor from the fish tray but remember it must bear the weight of the asparagus and skate.) Cut the remaining lime into 6 and add a segment to each plate. Spoon the lime and caper sauce over and around the fish.

Nicky Clarke

seabass baked in salt crust with greek salad

1kg coarse sea salt
1kg fine table salt
3 cloves garlic, finely chopped
about 15 bay leaves
1 wild seabass (tell your fishmongers you
    need one big enough for 4, and ask
    them to clean and prepare it for you)

FOR THE GREEK SALAD
rocket leaves
feta cheese, roughly cubed
black olives, pitted
tomatoes, chopped or sliced
red onion, thinly sliced
basil leaves, chopped or left whole
extra virgin olive oil and freshly squeezed
    lemon juice, to dress the salad

SERVES FOUR

A highlight of every summer is ordering this dish at my favourite restaurant, a little place overlooking the sea in Mallorca. But, perhaps rather foolishly, this was the first time I had ever tried to cook it myself! The single most important thing is to ensure that the salt is well packed, so the fish is completely sealed with no gaps. Contrary to expectations, the end result doesn't taste salty at all – just moist and, if all has gone well, deliciously flavoursome. I served this with Greek salad. My mother is from Greece and these are the ingredients she uses. Like all instinctive cooks, she doesn't measure anything but trusts her eye. You will have to do the same … but you can't really go wrong.

1 Preheat the oven to 220°C/Gas 7.

2 Mix the coarse sea salt and fine table salt together in a bowl. Add a little water to make it easier to work with. Lay out a salty base on a baking tray. Sprinkle the chopped garlic, about 5 bay leaves and some black pepper over the salt. To get a stronger 'bay leaf' flavour in the finished dish, twist the bay leaves to release their flavour.

3 Lay the fish on the salt, and put the rest of the bay leaves in the body cavity and on top of the fish. Be careful to tuck in the body cavity of the fish to prevent too much salt getting inside, then cover everything in salt (you can leave the head and tail salt-free if you like). Be sure to pack it tightly.

4 Bake the fish in the hot oven for 35–40 minutes.

5 Meanwhile, prepare the Greek salad by putting all the ingredients together according to eye and to taste. Toss in extra virgin olive oil and lemon juice. Season to taste.

6 Remove the fish from the oven and crack the salt crust. Peel back the skin of the fish and serve it at once.

Sue Thomas

vegetable moussaka

50g green or brown lentils
4–6 tbsp olive oil
1 onion, finely chopped
1 clove garlic, crushed
100g mushrooms, chopped
2–3 tbsp tomato purée
2 tsp dried oregano
½ tsp freshly grated nutmeg
2 medium aubergines, sliced
2–3 large potatoes, boiled and sliced
2 tomatoes, thickly sliced

FOR THE SAUCE
20g butter
1 tbsp flour
225ml milk
1 small egg
½ tsp mustard powder
75g Cheddar cheese, grated

SERVES FIVE

This is a good, unpretentious dish, nothing fussy about it, just tasty food you can relax around. To be honest, Wales isn't the easiest place in the world to be a vegetarian, and I had to overcome some initial scepticism from my guests. One of them, Ernie, was a real meat-eater, but at the end of the night he asked me for the recipe.

1 Preheat the oven to 180°C/Gas 4.

2 Pick the lentils over for sticks and stones, wash them thoroughly, then bring them to the boil in 500ml water. Cover and simmer for 40–45 minutes or until they are soft. When cooked, drain and reserve the liquid for stock.

3 Heat 2 tbsp of the oil in a frying pan and fry the onion and garlic gently so they remain translucent. Add the chopped mushrooms and cooked lentils and cook for a few more minutes, stirring well. Transfer to a bowl. Add a little of the reserved stock, the tomato purée and oregano to the bowl, and season well with the nutmeg, and salt and freshly ground black pepper.

4 Add 2 tbsp oil to the frying pan and fry the aubergine slices until soft, turning them over constantly, adding the remaining oil if needed. Put the slices onto a piece of kitchen paper to drain and let them cool.

5 Grease a 1.75-litre ovenproof dish and put in a layer of lentil and mushroom mixture, then a layer of aubergines, then of potato and tomato slices.

6 Next make the white sauce. Melt the butter in a small saucepan and stir in the flour. Cook the roux for 2–3 minutes. Pour on the milk and bring the sauce to the boil, stirring constantly. Simmer for 5 minutes and then allow to cool. Beat in the egg and season the sauce well with the mustard, and salt and pepper. Pour the sauce over the top of the casserole and sprinkle over the grated cheese.

7 Bake for 40 minutes until the cheese is golden brown and bubbling. Serve hot.

Lisa Quinton

chicken mafiosa

olive oil, for frying
5 chicken breasts
2–3 shallots, finely chopped
250g mixed mushrooms: chestnut, oyster
   and any wild mushrooms you like, sliced
   or whole, depending on size
chopped fresh tarragon, to taste
2 capfuls brandy
150ml double cream

I work as a waitress in a café, and this is one of our most popular dishes. It goes down a treat with kids too. It's easy, quick and delicious, though I adapted it slightly for *Come Dine With Me*, adding shallots and wild mushrooms, the more varied and adventurous the better. I find a quick slug of the brandy while cooking always goes down well too! I served this with roast potatoes, baby carrots and sugarsnap peas. For my roast potatoes, I parboil the potatoes, then coat in flour, sea salt and rosemary and roast in olive oil in a hot oven.

1 Heat some olive oil over a medium-high heat in a frying pan big enough to accommodate all the chicken without overlap, then add the chicken breasts and sear on both sides. Reduce the heat to medium, add the shallots and mushrooms, cover and allow the chicken to cook gently, stirring from time to time, until it is done: about 25 minutes.

2 Add fresh tarragon to taste, then turn up the heat to high and pour in the brandy. Allow to bubble briefly to burn off the alcohol. Pour in the cream, season to taste and allow to heat through until hot. Serve the chicken on warmed plates with the creamy sauce spooned over.

Jim Blythe

chicken in bahian sauce with manioc

6 tbsp palm oil
1 onion, chopped
120g creamed coconut
6 chicken breasts, thickly sliced
400g tin chopped tomatoes
chilli powder, to taste
3 cloves garlic, chopped
400g frozen prawns (king prawns are best, but it doesn't matter too much), thawed
1 manioc (cassava) root, about 1–1 ½ kg – note: raw manioc is poisonous: do not eat it raw, and make sure you wash your hands well before touching any other food!
oil, for deep-frying

I once had a Brazilian girlfriend – we had duty-frees with every date because she lived in Porto Alegre and I live in Cardiff. I first tasted this dish, or something very like it, at the foot of the Corcovado in Rio de Janeiro, where it was made by a street vendor. I invented a name for my version: galinha com molho baiano, Portuguese for 'chicken in Bahian sauce'. The recipe is actually based on West African cuisine. Slaves took their food culture with them to Brazil, where it evolved into Bahian cooking, popular throughout the country. Interestingly, manioc is South American, but it was transplanted to Africa where it became a staple crop (known as cassava).

1 Heat the palm oil in a large saucepan and gently fry the onion until soft. Add the block of coconut and allow it to melt. Then add the chicken, tomatoes, chilli and garlic, and season with salt. Cover and cook for about 20–25 minutes or until the chicken is done, checking the moisture level regularly and topping up with water if it starts to look dry. Add the prawns at the end of the cooking, bring back to a simmer, and serve.

2 Peel the manioc and cut it into 3cm cubes. (Wash your hands after touching it.) Boil until tender: test with a skewer as you would potatoes. Let the cubes cool, then deep-fry them just before serving so as to brown and crisp them. Serve with the Bahian chicken on warmed plates.

Mica Paris

rice and peas

1 tbsp olive oil
2 cloves garlic, finely chopped
3–4 spring onions, finely chopped
2 sprigs fresh thyme, leaves picked off
400g tin red kidney beans ('the peas'),
    drained and rinsed
250g Thai jasmine rice (or white basmati),
    rinsed
400ml tin coconut milk, shaken well
    before opening
25g butter

Fresh gungo peas (pigeon peas) are used when in season, but red kidney beans are usually the 'peas' of Jamaican rice and peas. I've given this an Asian twist by using jasmine rice, a long-grain sticky rice with a fragrant aroma that goes brilliantly with the chicken (see facing page).

1 Put the olive oil in a large saucepan, add the garlic, spring onions and thyme leaves, and cook gently until the onion is soft: about 2–3 minutes. Add the kidney beans and rice, and stir well. Pour in the coconut milk, then half fill the tin with water, swirl around to pick up the last of the coconut, and add that to the pan too. Stir to mix well, add the butter, cover and bring to the boil.

2 Season well, reduce the heat to VERY low and leave, covered, until the rice has softened and all the liquid has been absorbed: about 20 minutes. Check and stir from time to time – if it looks too dry add a little more hot water; if it looks too wet, uncover the pan. Test and adjust the seasoning, and serve.

Mica Paris

jamaican chicken

6 organic, skinless chicken thighs
1 lemon, halved
1 tsp Caribbean madras curry powder
2 cloves garlic, finely chopped
2 sprigs fresh thyme, leaves picked off
2 tbsp olive oil
2 green peppers, chopped
1 onion, finely chopped
1 tomato, chopped
1 sprig of flat-leaf parsley
hot chicken stock

SERVES SIX

Curried chicken is another classic Jamaican dish. It's worth using special Caribbean madras curry powder if you can find it, as it's quite different from the Indian variety, with more turmeric than usual. I marinate the chicken thighs overnight for best flavour. I call this a dangerous dish, as you just can't stop eating it!

1 Clean the chicken thighs in lemon water (using the halved lemons). In a small bowl, combine the curry powder, garlic and thyme with plenty of salt and freshly ground pepper, and rub this mixture over the chicken. Leave for 2 hours, or overnight if possible.

2 Heat the oil in a large pan over medium heat and fry the chicken on all sides until golden brown. Then lower the heat and add the green peppers, onion, tomato and parsley, and enough chicken stock to cover, before placing a lid on the pan and leaving to simmer for 20–25 minutes. Serve with the rice and peas.

Linda Barker

herb-crusted lamb with mint sauce

2 racks of lamb (6-chop)
4 slices stale bread
small bunch each of chives, mint and parsley
1 clove garlic
2–3 tbsp oil, such as olive

FOR THE MINT SAUCE
fresh mint
1 tsp sugar
white wine vinegar, to taste

SERVES FOUR

This dish can be adapted to any time of year – lamb will support most herbs, so I tend to work with whatever's in season. My guests all wanted their lamb cooked differently: those who wanted it well done got the end bits, while those who preferred their meat rarer were served the middle part of the joint. The perfect dish for a fussy set of guests! I served this with classic potatoes dauphinoise and a range of spring vegetables, which I blanched briefly ahead of time, then cooled and refrigerated, finishing them off by sautéing in butter just before serving.

1 Preheat the oven to 220°C/Gas 7. Process the bread, herbs and garlic into crumbs, season well, add the oil and process again briefly. Press the mixture over the skin side of the racks of lamb, then place in a roasting pan, crust uppermost, and roast for 20 minutes for rare, 30 minutes for medium and 40 minutes for well done. Slice into cutlets to serve.

2 For the sauce, chop the mint, add the sugar and 3 tbsp boiling water, then stir in a little vinegar to taste. Serve in a jug for your guests to help themselves.

Rebecca Hambley

lamb tagine with roasted vegetable couscous & red pepper harissa

LAMB TAGINE WITH PRUNES AND HONEY
2 tbsp ras el hanout
1 tsp ground ginger
½ tsp cayenne pepper
pinch of saffron threads
500ml beef stock
50g butter
800g boneless lamb, cut into 4cm cubes
2 onions, coarsely grated
3 cloves garlic, chopped
long stick cinnamon, about 10cm
3 small tomatoes, chopped
225g dried prunes
225g whole blanched almonds, sautéed
    in butter
2–3 tbsp honey
1 tsp ground cinnamon

I'd never tasted Moroccan food until a couple of years ago, when my dad took me to a restaurant and I was blown away by the range and subtlety of the flavours involved. The doors had opened on a whole new world. Tagine is a classic Moroccan dish, traditionally cooked in a heavy clay pot with a rounded bottom. Luckily, given the difficulty of balancing a real tagine on my electric hotplate, a casserole with a tight-fitting lid works just as well. As for the couscous, the important thing is to ensure it's not dry. If necessary, add a few drops of oil or lemon juice – whatever takes your fancy. For the harissa, I've replaced some of the chillies of the standard version with roasted red peppers for my milder one. As for the spice blend ras el hanout, you can buy it in any good supermarket or Middle-Eastern or North African food store.

Lamb tagine with prunes and honey
1 Whisk the ras el hanout, ginger, cayenne and saffron with plenty of salt and freshly ground black pepper into the stock. In a large tagine or a stockpot over a moderate heat, melt the butter, then add the lamb, onion and garlic and turn to coat them in the butter. Add the cinnamon stick and tomatoes, then pour over the scented stock and turn up the heat to high. When the liquid is almost boiling, reduce the heat to very low, cover and simmer until the lamb is tender: about 1½ hours.

2 Stir in the prunes, almonds, honey and ground cinnamon. Cover and simmer until the meat is very tender: about a further 30 minutes.

3 Uncover the pot, increase the heat to medium-high and cook, stirring occasionally, until the stew has slightly thickened: about a further 20 minutes.

a selection of vegetables for roasting, such
    as peppers, red onions, aubergines and
    courgettes, roughly chopped
extra virgin olive oil
500g couscous
pinch of saffron threads
400g tin chickpeas, drained
75g pine nuts, briefly toasted in the oven
    or under the grill
100g raisins
handful each of fresh coriander, flat-leaf
    parsley and mint, leaves finely chopped
1 tbsp harissa (see recipe)
125ml lemon juice

500g fresh or thawed frozen broad beans
100ml extra virgin olive oil
2 cloves garlic, crushed
1 red chilli, finely chopped
100g rocket, chopped
1 preserved lemon, finely chopped
juice of 1 lemon
fresh mint, finely chopped, to serve

2 red peppers, roasted, deseeded and peeled
1 small green/red chilli, chopped (with or
    without seeds according to taste)
1 tbsp paprika
5 cloves garlic
½ tsp ground cumin
1 tsp ground coriander
½ tsp caraway seeds
2 tbsp freshly squeezed lemon juice
1 tbsp chopped fresh mint (optional)
1 tsp salt
2 tbsp extra virgin olive oil

Roasted vegetable couscous

1 Preheat the oven to 200°C/Gas 6. Toss the vegetables in olive oil in a roasting dish, season well, then roast until tender and lightly browned on the edges: keep testing for tenderness and tossing the pan so the vegetables cook evenly. Remove from the oven and set aside.

2 Prepare the couscous according to packet instructions: it's usually twice the volume of (hot) water to couscous. Add the saffron, stir well and set aside, keeping the dish warm. Once the liquid has been absorbed, add all the remaining ingredients, including the roasted vegetables, and fork them through. Add some olive oil if the grains stick. Keep warm in a moderate oven until ready to serve.

Broad bean salad with preserved lemons

1 Briefly boil the broad beans, drain, cool, then remove the tough outer shell. Heat 1 tbsp of the olive oil in a pan over a medium heat, add the garlic and chilli and fry for a few minutes. Add the bright green broad beans, rocket, preserved lemon, lemon juice and the remaining oil. Simmer for 10 minutes and serve sprinkled with lots of fresh mint.

Not-so-spicy harissa

1 Place all the ingredients, except the oil, in a blender or food processor and whiz until smooth. With the motor running, add the oil in a steady stream to form a thick sauce. This sauce may be stored, covered, in the fridge for up to 3 weeks. Seal the top with a thin layer of olive oil to prevent the harissa turning brown.

John Santamaria

fillet of beef in wild mushroom sauce with potatoes dauphinoise & spinach

olive oil
1kg fillet of beef

FOR THE POTATOES DAUPHINOISE
775g potatoes, such as King Edward, peeled
butter
4 garlic cloves, finely chopped
500ml double cream

FOR THE MUSHROOM SAUCE
4 garlic cloves, finely chopped
2 shallots, finely chopped
1 fresh red chilli, finely chopped
1 handful fresh flat-leaf parsley, finely chopped
150g dried porcini mushrooms, soaked in cold
    water for 2 hours, drained and chopped
125g fresh crimini mushrooms, chopped
125g fresh shitake mushrooms, chopped
2 tbsp vermouth (Noilly Prat)
200ml double cream

FOR THE SPINACH
750g fresh spinach
butter

SERVES FOUR

The former Kensington restaurant called the Trattoo, which was run by my father, Giancarlo, inspired this. It always reminds me of happy times for my father when the restaurant was full of celebrities eating fillet of beef.

1 Preheat the oven to 200°C/Gas 6.

2 First prepare the dauphinoise. Boil the potatoes for about 10 minutes, then drain and leave in cold water until cool. Prepare an ovenproof dish by rubbing it with butter and scatter over the chopped garlic. Remove the potatoes from the water and slice finely and evenly, then layer into the dish, seasoning each layer. Pour the cream over. Set aside while you prepare the beef.

3 Pour some olive oil into the bottom of a deep roasting tray and place over a medium heat on the hob. Once the oil is quite hot, place the meat in the tray and sear for about 10 minutes, turning frequently. Then place both the meat in its tray and the dish of potatoes in the preheated oven and cook for 30 minutes.

4 After 30 minutes, remove the beef from the oven and set aside to rest. Give the potatoes another 10 minutes. While the beef is resting, make the mushroom sauce.

5 Heat some olive oil in a frying pan and cook the garlic, shallots and chilli until soft. Add the parsley and mushrooms and cook for about 5 minutes over a medium heat or until the mushrooms are tender. Add the vermouth and about 150ml of the double cream, allowing the sauce to thicken over a low heat. Add the rest of the cream if needed and leave on a low heat until you are ready to serve.

6 Just before you slice the beef and serve up the potatoes, place a large pan on a high heat, add the spinach leaves and a knob of butter and wilt for 2 minutes.

7 Spoon the mushroom sauce over the beef and serve immediately with the potatoes and spinach.

Darren Frame

barbecued ribs with home-made barbecue sauce & egg-fried rice

6 racks of baby back pork ribs

FOR THE BBQ SAUCE
8 tbsp dark brown soft sugar
2 tbsp vinegar
340g bottle of tomato sauce
½ × 430g bottle of BBQ sauce (optional
  – can use more tomato sauce)
½ 150ml bottle of sweet chilli sauce
1 tsp garlic powder
1 tsp 'lazy ginger' (ginger in a jar)
splash of soy sauce
splash of Tabasco
1 tsp mild curry powder, or to taste

FOR THE EGG-FRIED RICE
125g long-grain rice
2 onions, chopped
vegetable oil, for frying
handful of mangetout
4 tbsp sweetcorn
4 tbsp garden peas
soy sauce
3 eggs, beaten

SERVES FOUR

Taken from an old recipe given to me by my nan, this sauce really hits the spot. Although pork ribs might not be everyone's first thought for a main course, my friends can't get enough of them. They are easily pre-prepared, and relatively cheap too. Make them as spicy or mild as you like and whack them on a serving dish – no chance of getting lost in the kitchen cooking all night.

1 Preheat the oven to 180°C/Gas 4. Chop the racks into separate ribs and lay them out in a 2.5cm-deep baking tray. Pour boiling water all over the ribs so there is about 5mm water in the tray. Cover with foil and cook on the top shelf of the oven for 2–3 hours. This steams the ribs and makes them VERY tender. Check from time to time and top up the tray with boiling water if it's getting dry.

2 Meanwhile, make the sauce. Put the sugar in a large saucepan with just enough hot water to melt it, then season with salt and pepper and add the vinegar. Stir well and bring to a simmer. Pour in the tomato sauce and stir well, then add the barbecue sauce and half a bottle of sweet chilli sauce (more if you want the sauce spicy). Add the garlic powder and lazy ginger, then a good splash of soy sauce and Tabasco. Heat through until the sauce is lightly simmering, stirring well continuously. Add curry power until you get the desired taste, then continue to

simmer, stirring. Turn the heat off and leave the sauce to cool: this gives the flavours time to develop. It's also difficult to dip ribs in a hot sauce.

3 Take the ribs out of the oven, remove the foil and pour off the water. Take out the ribs, place them on a rack and leave them to dry for 10–15 minutes. Dry ribs hold the BBQ sauce better. Wipe the tray clean. Reduce the oven temperature to 150°C/Gas 2.

4 When the ribs are dry, dip them individually into the BBQ sauce and return to the cleaned baking tray. Put them back in the oven and cook for 30 minutes. This makes the sauce go sticky.

5 For the egg-fried rice, boil the rice in plenty of water until just cooked – do not allow it to go too soggy! Drain the rice and pour boiling water over to remove starch. Leave to drain well and almost dry out.

6 Stir-fry the onions in a little hot oil in a frying pan until softened. Add the mangetout, sweetcorn and peas and season with a little soy sauce. Stir-fry for 1–2 minutes.

7 Pour a little oil in a wok and heat it up. Add the eggs and cook, stirring continuously, until they are scrambled but still light and fluffy: this takes a matter of seconds. Stir the rice into the eggs and add plenty of soy sauce. Add the vegetables and stir through. Transfer to a large warmed serving bowl.

8 When the ribs are done, transfer to a serving platter. Serve, and enjoy!

Jane Bates

pirates' planked steak, aka johnny depp

1 clove garlic, halved
olive oil
fresh herbs of your choice
5 thick fillet steaks, about 125g each
150g Boursin cheese with garlic and herbs
balsamic vinegar

SERVES FIVE

This is such an unusual and fun dish to make – but first you need to source your own piece of seasoned oak. I've used the same one for over twenty years now. Make sure the wood is really hot before putting the meat on, then turn the oven down and let the wood do the cooking. Personally, I like my steak medium rare: 5 minutes on one side, then 10–15 minutes on the other. It sounds a lot for steak, but the wood makes sure it cooks nicely and slowly. The end result is smoky in flavour and deliciously tender. I served this with on a bed of mashed potatoes with finely chopped spring onions, with griddled asparagus and butter-glazed carrots on the side. I don't recommend making this in a gas oven, however well-seasoned your piece of oak is; my oven's electric.

1 Preheat the oven to 250°C. Prepare the 'plank' by rubbing it with garlic and oil and covering it with fresh herbs. Place it in the hot oven for 30 minutes.

2 Place the steaks on top of the plank and cook for 5 minutes. Turn over and cook for a further 10–15 minutes, or to taste. Just before serving, top with a knob of Boursin cheese and drizzle balsamic vinegar over.

Linda Lusardi

rainbow peppercorn steak with stuffed baked potatoes

4 thick fillet steaks, about 125g each
oil, for frying
2–3 tbsp rainbow peppercorns,
    lightly crushed
2–3 tbsp brandy
1½ tbsp Dijon mustard
300ml whipping cream
half a lemon
Worcestershire sauce
1 heaped tsp chopped parsley

FOR THE STUFFED POTATOES
2 large baking potatoes, baked until soft
3 onions, finely chopped
3 large tomatoes, finely chopped
handful mushrooms, finely chopped
125g butter
125g Cheddar cheese

SERVES FOUR

The idea for these potatoes came when I was at the end of my tether trying to get my kids to eat their vegetables. I came up with the idea of hiding their carrots and broccoli in amongst the mashed-up potato and melted cheese! The fact they slip down so nicely is almost an added bonus. This is also a great way to use up any leftover vegetables from the day before.

1 First prepare the stuffed potatoes. Cut the baked potatoes in half and scrape the insides into a large bowl. Keep the skins. Fry the onions, tomatoes and mushrooms in a frying pan in a little of the butter until softened. Add to the bowl with the potato flesh and stir in the rest of the butter. Fill the skins with the mixture and sprinkle the top with the grated cheese.

2 Fry the steaks to taste (see, for example, the facing page) in a small amount of oil in a frying pan. Remove the steaks from the pan (put on a plate and wrap in foil to keep them warm) and heat the peppercorns, brandy, mustard and cream in the meat juices. Simmer for 5–6 minutes until thickened.

3 Meanwhile, put the stuffed baked potatoes under the grill until the cheese has melted.

4 Add a pinch of salt, a squeeze of lemon and a splash of Worcestershire to the peppercorn sauce. Serve the steaks with the sauce on top, sprinkled with the parsley, and the stuffed baked potatoes alongside.

James Paley

fillet steak with mushroom, pancetta & port sauce & parsnip crisps

2 parsnips
olive oil and butter, for frying
4 best quality thick fillet steaks (about 125g each)
2 medium shallots, finely chopped
2 cloves garlic, finely chopped
2 slices pancetta, in thin strips
200g small wild mushrooms, roughly chopped
small glass of port
125ml beef stock (made with a stock cube if you like)

Wild mushrooms have a nutty, woody taste, much stronger than the standard button mushroom. Combined with the strong, salty flavour of the pancetta, this doesn't really need extra seasoning. You can use red wine seasoned with a little balsamic vinegar instead of port, but the port gives it a sweeter, richer flavour. By all means grill the steak if you prefer, but personally I always pan-fry, to keep the flavour and juices in. Serve with chips, roasted potatoes or potatoes dauphinoise.

1 First make the parsnip crisps. Cut the parsnips into a heap of thin shavings using a potato peeler. Shallow-fry the shavings in olive oil until golden brown (you may need to do this in batches). Drain on kitchen paper and set aside. They crisp up after cooking.

2 Heat a large, heavy-based frying pan over high heat until very hot. Put a little oil and butter in the hot frying pan, then add the steaks and straight away turn the heat down a little. Cook for 2–4 minutes each side, or longer, according to preference. Season with freshly ground black pepper. Remove to a warm dish and cover with foil to retain the heat.

3 Fry the shallots and garlic in the pan the steaks were cooked in, until the shallots pick up some colour. Add the pancetta and mushrooms and sauté these for about 2 minutes. Deglaze the pan with the port, add the stock and any juices that have run from the cooked steaks and reduce until the sauce begins to thicken. Taste and season if necessary.

4 Serve the steaks on warmed plates with the sauce poured over and the crisps on the side.

Nick Cooper

salted beef with home-made horseradish sauce

a piece of brisket on the bone, about 5kg

FOR THE BRINE
1kg sea salt
1 tsp black peppercorns
1 tsp juniper berries
3 bay leaves
sprig of fresh thyme
25g saltpetre (optional)
5 litres water

FOR THE STOCK
2 carrots
1 stick celery
2 bay leaves
1 onion
bouquet garni
black peppercorns
1 clove garlic

FOR THE HORSERADISH SAUCE
fresh horseradish root
mustard seeds
crème fraiche (full fat)

I love salt beef, and it is easy and rewarding to make. It's the ultimate thrift food as it's best made with one of the cheapest cuts of beef, namely the brisket, which contains layers of fat that give the salt beef a delicious grainy texture when carved. It's a good-natured dish to make and is not sensitive to critical timing. It can be pickled for between one and two weeks and cooked for hours, and will always be good. This dish is wonderful hot with horseradish and mash, and excellent the next day with crusty bread and good English mustard.

1 Bring to the boil all the ingredients for the brine, simmer for 1 minute, skim off any scum that rises and allow to cool thoroughly, then chill.

2 Place the beef in a non-metallic container, pour the brine over, then store in the fridge for 7–10 days.

3 Take the beef out of the brine and soak in fresh water for 24 hours before cooking, changing the water at least once to remove excess salt.

4 Place the meat in a large pan, add the stock ingredients and water to cover and bring to a gentle boil, then reduce the heat and poach very gently for about 3 hours. The water should not boil; it must barely simmer.

5 For the horseradish sauce, wash and peel the horseradish root. Grate what is left as finely as you can and mix with a slightly smaller quantity of crème fraiche: you want about 60/40 horseradish to cream. Pound some mustard seeds to a paste in a mortar and add to the sauce to taste. (Or use English mustard from a jar.)

6 Remove the salted beef from the simmering stock, carve into thick slices and serve immediately with the horseradish sauce.

Dan Churchill

wild boar in red wine sauce

1.2kg wild boar haunch joint, boned
    and rolled
240ml olive oil
5 sprigs rosemary
5 cloves garlic, crushed
5 juniper berries
20 green beans
10 fresh baby carrots
a handful of wild mushrooms
5 rashers streaky bacon
2½ not-too-ripe pears, sliced
a large glass of full-bodied red wine,
    such as Barolo (175ml)
1 tsp sugar
1 pork stock cube

SERVES FIVE

Wild boar is an amazing meat, low in cholesterol, high in protein and wonderfully flavoursome. Any good butcher should be able to order it for you or you can buy it online. Either way, you should ask for the joint to be boned and rolled. Some people think of Italian food as being expensive and fancy, but this is Tuscan cuisine, real down-to-earth peasant's fare. I sometimes think the Tuscans could make a delicious meal out of a pair of old shoes, provided they were marinated for long enough in a full-bodied, rich Italian red wine! Serve this with potatoes.

1 Put the wild boar in a flameproof casserole dish, pour the olive oil over and add the rosemary, garlic and juniper berries. Marinate in the fridge for 1 hour.

2 Preheat the oven to 190°C/Gas 5. Remove the boar from the fridge and bring to room temperature, then roast for 1½ hours.

3 Meanwhile, lightly boil the green beans and baby carrots. Thirty minutes before the end of cooking, add the carrots along with the wild mushrooms to the casserole dish containing the boar. Fifteen minutes before the end of cooking, wrap 4 green beans in each rasher of bacon and add to the dish, along with the pears.

4 Remove the boar from the oven and transfer it to a warmed plate. Arrange the carrots, pears, mushrooms and bacon-wrapped beans around the meat.

5 Pour away excess oil from the casserole dish, and discard the garlic, rosemary and juniper berries. Pour in the red wine and add the sugar and stock cube. Bring to the boil over a moderate heat on the hob and allow to bubble until slightly reduced. Slice the boar, pour the red wine sauce over and bring to the table.

Daniel Fletcher

duck (magret de canard) à la pêche et à l'orange

5 duck breasts, skin on
4 oranges, peeled and cut into segments
4 peaches, peeled and cut into chunks
80g sugar
5 large potatoes, quartered
4 tbsp sunflower oil
2 sprigs rosemary
250g sugarsnap peas

This is similar to duck à l'orange, but I've added peach, which I think really complements the other flavours. I chose duck because I wanted the main course to feel a bit special, and while duck isn't as posh as some people think, it still feels like a bit of treat. On the night I served this with sugarsnap peas and roast potatoes, which should have made a nice simple accompaniment to the rich sweetness of the duck and the fruit. However, I managed to burn the roast potatoes – something probably best avoided!

1 Rinse the duck breasts and pat dry with kitchen paper.

2 Put the orange and peach pieces and the sugar in a saucepan with 150ml water, bring to the boil then simmer for 20 minutes until you have a runny jam-like consistency, in which the lumps of fruit can still be seen. Set aside, keeping it warm.

3 Preheat the oven to 200°C/Gas 6.

4 Boil the potatoes until just cooked. Drain in a colander, then shake the colander from side to side to fluff the potatoes up a little. Place on a baking tray, add the oil and rosemary, and turn the potatoes in the oil to coat them. Roast for about 40–50 minutes or until golden.

5 Place the duck skin-side down in a cold frying pan and place on full heat. Cook for 5–6 minutes until the skin has gone crisp, then turn over and cook for a further 6 minutes for a pink finish. Boil the sugarsnap peas for 1–2 minutes.

6 Serve the duck with the sauce, the roasted potatoes and the sugarsnap peas.

Simone Burns

ling ling's chilli pork & white radish salad

500g leg of pork, without bone but fat
  still on, tied

FOR THE WHITE RADISH SALAD
1 large white Chinese radish (mooli)
1 tbsp salt
1 tbsp rice vinegar
½ bunch spring onions, finely chopped
½ tbsp sesame oil
1 tbsp vegetable oil

FOR THE SAUCE
6 tbsp soy sauce
2 tbsp sesame oil
1cm red chilli, finely chopped
2 tbsp fresh lemon juice
1 tsp finely chopped garlic
4 tbsp finely chopped coriander

SERVES FIVE

At a noodle shop in Manhattan's Chinatown, after I'd lost
my purse, I struck up a deal to slave in the dish pit to pay
for my soup. Before I knew it, several hours had passed
and there were no dishes left. In gratitude the owner
served me a pork dish that would haunt me for years …
until the day I met Ling Ling and she cooked it for me –
salvation at last. This is it. Serve with egg noodles.

1 Place the tied-up leg of pork in a pot and cover with
cold water. Cover with a lid and bring slowly to the boil,
then reduce the heat and simmer for about 30 minutes.
Turn off the heat and leave the pot on the hob for another
2 hours.

2 Peel the radish into long thin strips with a potato peeler.
You should end up with mountain of fine strips. Put in a
large bowl, sprinkle with the salt and mix well using your
hands. Cover and leave for at least 2 hours.

3 Mix all the ingredients for the sauce and place in a
serving bowl. Taste and adjust seasoning if necessary.

4 Take the pork from the water, remove the string and
thinly slice. You can choose to leave the fat on. Arrange
on a serving plate.

5 Rinse the radish with fresh water and drain. Add the
vinegar, spring onions and some freshly ground black
pepper. Take a big serving plate and pile up the radish as
high as you can. Stick two chopsticks into the pile, because
it looks good, and you need them in a moment.

6 Heat the sesame and vegetable oils in a small saucepan
until hot (but not smoking). Bring the salad to the table.
Pour the hot oil over the salad so that it sizzles, and use
the chopsticks to toss the salad.

7 The way you eat it is like this: take chopsticks, pick up
a slice of pork, dip it in sauce, put it in your mouth …

Seamus Farrelly

fillet of beef with duchess potatoes & creamed leeks & runner beans

6 tbsp olive oil, plus extra to rub
    into the beef
800g centre-cut beef fillet
50g butter
a few sprigs of thyme

FOR THE DUCHESS POTATOES
3 large potatoes
60g unsalted butter
100ml double cream
pinch of nutmeg

FOR THE CREAMED LEEKS
    AND RUNNER BEANS
2 medium leeks, finely chopped
150g runner beans, stringed and
    cut into slices on the diagonal
100ml double cream
1 tsp English mustard
1 tsp hazelnut or vegetable oil
handful of fresh chervil or parsley,
    chopped

SERVES FOUR

The art here is being brave enough to cook the meat until you could cut it with the side of your plate, it's so tender. The marriage of the textures of the meat and the creamy potatoes browned slightly in the oven gets the job done. This is one of my favourite meals. My friends and family always ask for it on special occasions.

1 Preheat the oven to 230°C/Gas 8.

2 Start by rubbing olive oil firmly into and all over the beef and seasoning generously with salt and pepper. Then sear the beef. Place an ovenproof frying pan over a high heat and add the oil. When the oil is hot, place the beef in the pan and sear each side for 1–1½ minutes. Add the butter and thyme and transfer to a high shelf in the oven. Roast the beef for 30 minutes for rare, turning occasionally to ensure even cooking and basting with the cooking juices. Turn the oven off, but if you like beef to be medium or well done, leave it in the oven for between 10 and 20 minutes. If you like it rare, remove it at once.

3 When the meat has been cooked to your taste and removed from the oven, place an inverted spoon on the pan. Using tongs, place the beef on top of the spoon to rest, so that air can circulate around it. Let it sit for a few minutes.

4 For the duchess potatoes, cook the potatoes in a pan of salted boiling water until soft. Drain and return to the pan and mash with the butter, cream and nutmeg, and salt and pepper to taste, until smooth. Transfer the creamy mash to a piping bag with a large nozzle and pipe rounds on a non-stick baking tray. (They can be prepared ahead to this point.) Bake in the oven for 5–6 minutes or until crisp and golden.

5 Put the leeks and beans into a saucepan and cover with water. Cook over a gentle heat, checking and stirring regularly, until they have softened: 5–7 minutes. Strain off any liquid and return the leeks and beans to the pan with the cream, mustard and oil. Season with a pinch of sea salt and lots of freshly ground black pepper. Cook for a few minutes more. (They can be prepared ahead to this point.) Reheat before serving if necessary, and sprinkle the chervil or parsley over at the last moment.

6 If you like, carve the beef at the table and serve the potatoes and vegetables in warmed serving dishes.

Ronnie Masters

tournedos on celeriac & potato rosti with a wild mushroom stroganoff

5 beef tournedos, about 150g each
olive oil

FOR THE ROSTI
120g potatoes, such as Maris Piper
120g celeriac
60g butter
2 tbsp oil

FOR THE STROGANOFF
60g butter
2 shallots, finely chopped
125g tub fresh oyster mushrooms, chopped
15g dried porcini mushrooms, soaked for 30
    minutes in hot water, drained and chopped
¼ tsp paprika
2–3 capfuls brandy, according to taste
60ml white wine
60ml double cream
freshly squeezed lemon juice and freshly
    chopped parsley, to serve

SERVES FIVE

The success of this dish is all in the quality of the beef, so buy the best you can afford. By searing the meat and preparing the stroganoff in advance, this is a perfect, stress-free dinner party main course. My advice when serving delicious tender beef is to go as rare as you dare!

1 You can make the stroganoff in advance. Melt the butter in a frying pan, add the shallots and fry gently until softened. Add the mushrooms and paprika and sauté for 3–4 minutes, then increase the heat, pour in the brandy (to taste) and allow to bubble and reduce for 1–2 minutes. Add the white wine and let that bubble and reduce, then lower the heat, add the cream and simmer gently for about 8 minutes. Season to taste with salt and pepper. Just before serving, reheat and add a good squeeze of lemon juice.

2 Preheat the oven to 200°C/Gas 6. Rub the beef tournedos all over with olive oil and season well with salt and freshly ground black pepper. Place a non-stick, ovenproof pan over high heat and quickly sear the beef on both sides until caramelized. Then transfer to the oven and roast for 6–8 minutes. Set aside for 10 minutes before serving.

3 To make the rosti, grate the potato and place in a cloth. Squeeze out the liquid, then put the potato in a mixing bowl. Peel and grate the celeriac and add to the grated potato. Season to taste. Heat half the butter and all the oil in a non-stick frying pan over a medium heat. When sizzling, put in the potato and celeriac and press down firmly. Keep pressing down so that the strands come together into a cake. Cook for 10 minutes. Melt the remaining butter on top of the rosti. Turn over carefully using a spatula, or by inverting the pan onto a plate and then sliding the rosti back into the pan. Cook the other side until well browned.

4 Cut the rosti into portions and serve with the tournedos on top and the stroganoff on the side. Garnish with parsley.

Desserts

Jim Blythe

glazed pears with coffee cream

6 firm ripe Williams (or other) pears
135g packet lime or lemon jelly
cherries or grapes (optional)
284ml tub extra-thick cream
1 tsp instant coffee powder
4 tsp sugar
5–6 tbsp whisky

SERVES SIX

I got the basic idea for this on the Orient Express. We were served a beautifully decorated steamed pear for dessert, and I had the idea of glazing it with lime jelly and adding extra fruit in jelly cubes. It's all prepared before the guests arrive, so if you're feeling the worse for wear after a few glasses of wine, you can still wow the diners. The idea for the coffee cream came as I was about to serve the dessert on the night of the show, and it was a risk that paid off.

1 Peel the pears. Steam or poach them until they are tender but not mushy (how long this takes will depend on how ripe they are, so keep testing them by pushing the tip of a knife into the base), then put them somewhere cool until they are absolutely cold – if you don't cool them thoroughly the jelly won't stick.

2 Make the jelly according to the instructions on the packet, but instead of making it up to 570ml, make 500ml, because the jelly will absorb some water from the fruit.

3 Quarter the pears and remove the core. Arrange on each individual plate, then spoon the jelly gently over to form a glaze. Set aside and allow to set for 1–2 hours.

4 If you have some jelly left over, put cherries or grapes into ice-cube trays, pour in the remaining jelly and allow it to set. This makes jelly cubes to add to the glazed pears.

5 Just before serving, put the cream into a bowl, add the coffee, sugar and whisky, then use a balloon whisk to beat the cream to a thick consistency. Serve alongside the glazed pears.

Bill Buckley

spiced orange chocolate cheesecake

200g dark chocolate digestive biscuits
50g butter, melted
2 × 100g bars of Green and Black's organic
   Maya Gold (spiced orange) chocolate
426ml double cream (1 large and 1 small tub)
250g full-fat cream cheese, such as Philadelphia
250g mascarpone
slug of Cointreau or Grand Marnier
2 oranges
a little caster or icing sugar

If you like, use half and freeze the rest for a future dinner party; it freezes beautifully. Brilliantly easy due to the chocolate, orange and spiciness all coming from one ingredient!

1 Whiz the biscuits in a food processor until they resemble breadcrumbs. Pour in the melted butter and whiz again to amalgamate. Grease a 20cm springform baking tin. Press the biscuit mixture down firmly to cover the base evenly. Refrigerate while you make the topping.

2 Break the chocolate into small pieces in a bowl. Put the bowl over a pan of barely simmering water until it starts to melt. Take it off and set it aside until it melts completely. You can stir it once or twice to help the process, but be gentle and don't overdo it. Cool slightly.

3 Gently beat two-thirds (284ml) of the cream, the cream cheese and mascarpone in a bowl until well combined. Stir in the melted chocolate. Spoon over the base and refrigerate for at least 3 hours, preferably overnight.

4 When ready to serve, whip the remaining cream and stir in the liqueur. Finely grate the orange peel and mix the threads of zest with a little sugar. Peel and segment the fruit.

5 Run a knife round the edge of the cheesecake, then release the springform tin. (Freeze half if you don't want to use it all at once.) Cut thin wedges of cheesecake and serve each one with a blob of cream topped with a few shreds of the candied zest and 2 or 3 orange segments on the side.

Christopher Biggins

auntie vi's trifle

2 tbsp custard powder
2 tbsp sugar
1 pint (568ml) full-cream milk
6 shop-bought sponge squares
6 tbsp raspberry jam
sherry, to taste
284ml whipping cream
walnut halves, to decorate
cherries, to decorate (fresh, glacé
    or morello, according to taste)

SERVES FOUR TO SIX

Good old Great-auntie Vi taught me how to do this – every boy should know how to make a perfect trifle. Talk about comfort food! I don't put fruit into my trifles because I don't like it, but I do like to saturate the sponge in a generous amount of sherry. I would normally make this the day before a dinner party so that the custard is nice and set.

1 In a medium-sized bowl, mix the custard powder and sugar to a smooth paste with 2 tablespoons of the milk. Bring the rest of the milk almost to the boil, then pour onto the custard mix, stirring well. Return the custard to the saucepan and bring to the boil over a gentle heat, stirring continuously, until thick enough to coat the spoon. Remove from the heat and set aside to cool, stirring from time to time to prevent a thick skin forming.

2 Halve the sponge squares and sandwich together with the jam. Arrange in the bottom of a beautiful glass bowl. Pour the sherry over the sponges – I like the sponge completely soaked, but you can adjust according to taste. Cover with the cooled custard and put in the fridge for several hours or overnight.

3 Just before serving, whip the cream until stiff, then layer on top of the custard. Decorate with walnuts and cherries, and serve.

Lisa Quinton

apple crumble with home-made cinnamon ice cream

2–3 Bramley apples, peeled and chopped
caster sugar, to taste
½ tsp ground cinnamon
sprinkling of desiccated coconut
250g crumble mix

FOR THE ICE CREAM
225ml milk
1 cinnamon stick
3 egg yolks
100g caster sugar
1 tsp ground cinnamon
450ml double cream

SERVES FIVE

We've eaten this in our family for as long as I can remember. What sets it apart from a normal crumble is the coconut, my personal twist on a classic dish. But the real star is the cinnamon ice cream. You need an ice-cream maker for this. Remember to allow plenty of time for it to set firm in the freezer – I've been caught out this way a few times. But if the worst comes to the worst, just serve it up as an equally delicious cinnamon cream, and no one will be any the wiser!

1 First make the ice cream. Bring the milk to the boil with the cinnamon stick, then set aside to cool down and for the milk to become infused with the cinnamon.

2 Whisk together the egg yolks and sugar until pale and thick, then add the ground cinnamon. Add the cream and cooled-down milk (discarding the cinnamon stick) and whisk together. Cool down in the fridge and finish in an ice-cream maker, then transfer to the freezer, in a suitable container, to set firm. Remove from the freezer about 20 minutes before serving with the hot apple crumble.

3 Preheat the oven to 200°C/Gas 6.

4 Put the apple in a lightly buttered baking dish, such as Pyrex, and scatter with sugar to taste – some like apples quite tart, others like them sweet – and the cinnamon. Stir the coconut into the crumble mix and sprinkle over the top to cover evenly. Cook until golden brown on top and the apple is bubbling away underneath: about 30 minutes. Allow to cool off a little, then serve warm with a scoop or two of cinnamon ice cream.

Benito Gundin

almond & pear tart

FOR THE PASTRY
400g plain flour
200g slightly salted butter
large pinch of salt
5 tbsp water, more if necessary

FOR THE REST OF THE TART
400g sugar and 400ml water to make
    a syrup (any type of sugar would do)
3 large, almost ripe pears (Williams pears
    are good)
juice of 1 lemon
300g caster sugar
300g unsalted butter, at room temperature
3 organic free-range eggs
300g ground almonds
crushed almonds, to garnish (optional)
vanilla or crème anglaise ice cream, to serve

SERVES SIX

I hadn't made this before – breaking dinner-party rule number one! – as I rarely cook desserts, so I found the whole thing quite challenging. But the end result surprised even myself. It was exquisite, and probably the key reason behind my victory. This recipe was provided by my friend, Steven McCallum, who is a fantastic chef. Buy really good vanilla or crème anglaise ice cream to serve it with, or make your own, like I did, using a recipe by Gordon Ramsay – who's another fantastic chef but not a friend of mine!

1 Mix the flour with the butter and salt until it looks like sand. Add the water and mix thoroughly. Make a ball, wrap it in cling film and keep it in the fridge for about 30 minutes.

2 Bring the sugar and water to the boil in a saucepan to make the syrup. In the meantime, peel the pears, halve them and remove the stem and seeds of the fruit. Let the syrup boil for 2 minutes, then add the lemon juice and the pears. Boil until the pears turn a brownish colour and you can easily cut them with a knife. Take the cooked pears out of the pan, using a slotted spoon because the sugar syrup is hellishly hot, and let them cool at room temperature.

3 Preheat the oven to 170°C/Gas 3. In a big bowl, place the caster sugar and unsalted butter and mix thoroughly with the help of an electric mixer. Add the eggs to the mixture and mix all together. Finally add the almonds and keep mixing to a smooth consistency.

4 Roll the pastry to a thickness of 3mm and place it in a greased, loose-bottomed fluted flan tin. You should have plenty of pastry left over, which you can save for another dish. Press the pastry gently into the edges of the tin. Pour the almond mixture over the pastry and arrange the 6 pear halves on top. For extra chic, slice each pear half as shown in the picture.

5 Bake for about 45minutes until golden brown and fragrant.

6 Cut the tart into 6 pieces with a pear half in each. Serve with the ice cream, and garnish with almonds if you like.

Nick Cooper

summer pudding with home-made berry ice cream

FOR THE ICE CREAM
800g berries or soft fruit of your choice
125g sugar, plus extra, to taste, for the fruit
4 large free-range egg yolks
568ml tub double cream

FOR THE SUMMER PUDDING
any combination of blackcurrants, redcurrants,
    raspberries, strawberries, blueberries,
    blackberries – whatever you like and
    whatever's in season
sugar, to taste
cassis (optional)
loaf of day-old white bread

SERVES FIVE

Summer pudding is brilliant. It is easy to make, tastes amazing and will always impress when you serve it. To me it really does sum up all the great flavours of summer.

1 Put the berries you've chosen to flavour your ice cream with into a saucepan with sugar to taste, and cook over a gentle heat for 2–3 minutes. Set aside to cool. Make a light syrup by dissolving 125g sugar in 150ml water over a gentle heat. (Don't allow to change colour.) Take off the heat and set aside to cool. Beat the egg yolks until smooth and mousse-like. Beat the cooled syrup into the egg yolks, then beat in the cream. Pass the cooled fruit through a sieve to get a fine purée free from pips, then beat this into the cream, egg and syrup mix. Churn in a ice-cream maker. Freeze until ready to use (remove from the freezer 20 minutes before serving).

2 To make the pudding, you simply need enough of your chosen fruit to fill a pudding basin of your chosen size. Pick over, wash and drain the fruit. Put into a saucepan with sugar to taste, or no sugar at all if the fruit is really fresh and summer-ripe, and cook over a gentle heat for 2–3 minutes. If using currants, they should have burst and released their juice. Set aside to cool, adding cassis if you want to.

3 Slice the bread thinly and remove the crusts. Very lightly butter the pudding basin to help the bread stick. Carefully line the basin with slices of bread, cutting misshapes to fill in any gaps and pressing the bread together to seal it.

4 Strain the fruit and reserve the extra juice. Spoon the fruit into the bread-lined bowl until full then cover the top with more bread. Cover with a plate or saucer and put a heavy weight on top. Leave to set in the fridge at least overnight or even for 2 days. Put the reserved juice in a screw-top jar in the fridge too.

5 Turn out onto a plate to serve. Pour the reserved juice over any white bits that are showing, if you like. Serve with the home-made berry ice cream.

Sandra Brooks

raspberry almond charlotte rousses

2 × 175g packets almond sponge fingers
    (you might not need them all)
½ tumbler of Amaretto
284ml fresh whipping cream
200g fresh raspberries
pouring cream, to serve (optional)

SERVES FOUR

I've been using this recipe since the 1970s, and I've actually made a lot of money out of it. Back in the day I was an executive for Tupperware, and I'd serve this up at every party I hosted. It would go down so well that all the ladies would buy the necessary mould. I've made loads of different versions, using Swiss roll, chocolate mousse, pears, mandarins – just unleash your creativity and let yourself go!

1 Rinse a large bowl or Tupperware mould in cold water. Cutting the sponge fingers in half, dip them into the Amaretto, one at a time, and place upright around the mould. Then place a layer of dry sponge fingers at the bottom, cutting them to fit.

2 Whip the cream until thick. Put a layer of raspberries into the mould, and then a layer of whipped cream. Repeat the layers (reserving some raspberries for decoration), and finish off with a layer of dry sponge fingers. Seal the mould to extract the air and push everything downwards. (If your mould doesn't have a lid, use a piece of greaseproof paper and an appropriately sized plate.) Chill for at least 6 hours in the fridge.

3 Invert the pudding onto a serving plate to serve. Decorate with the reserved raspberries, and serve with a jug of pouring cream on the table, if you like.

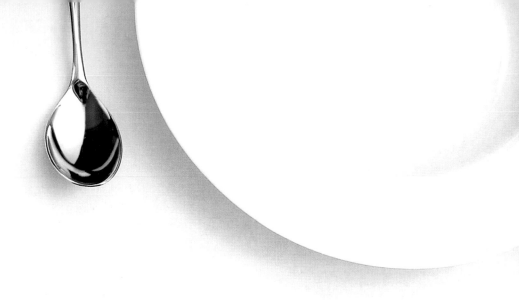

Laura Rojales

leche flan

8 tsp syrup, such as golden syrup
8 egg yolks
1 tin condensed milk (397g)
1 tin evaporated milk (410g)
100g sugar
1 tsp vanilla essence
finely grated zest of 1 lemon

SERVES EIGHT

Leche flan is a famous, traditional Filipino dessert. What better way to finish off my delicious meal, I thought, than something from my home country?

1 Preheat the oven to 190°C/Gas 5.

2 Put 1 tsp syrup into each ramekin or other small ovenproof mould (125–150ml capacity).

3 Beat the egg yolks, condensed milk, evaporated milk, sugar and vanilla together. Keep stirring and mixing until the sugar granules are melted, then strain into a clean bowl. Add the lemon zest.

4 Pour the mixture into the containers and cover each one with foil. Place in a baking tray, which you half fill with boiling water, then steam in the oven for 35 minutes. Remove from the oven, allow to cool, then refrigerate until cold. To serve, run a knife around the edges to loosen, then invert onto dessert plates.

Daniel Fletcher

french summer fruit pudding with mascarpone

500g mixed fruits of the forest (berries)
100g sugar
2 × 175g packets sponge fingers (you might
    not need them all)
strawberries and mint, to decorate
200g mascarpone cheese, to serve

This pudding – *dessert aux baies des bois, servi avec de la mascarpone* – is an old French recipe passed down from my grandmother to my mother. It has a little in common with English summer pudding. You could easily use ice cream instead of mascarpone, but I feel the creamy texture of the mascarpone cheese cuts nicely through the sharper fruit flavours. You can make one large pudding or six small ones.

1 Put the mixed fruit in a pan with the sugar and 100ml water, bring to the boil then simmer for about 10 minutes. Take off the heat and set aside.

2 Cutting the sponge fingers to fit, arrange them around the sides and base of a soufflé dish or 6 small ramekins, keeping some for the top. Pour in the mixed fruits, making sure the liquid goes all over the sponge fingers. Finish off by placing the reserved biscuits on top. Put some greaseproof paper over the top and weight down gently, such as with a plate or a board. Leave to set in the fridge for at least 2 hours.

3 Turn onto a serving plate, decorate with strawberries and mint leaves, and serve with the mascarpone on the side.

Sam Mallett

raspberry sorbet & vegan soya ice cream

FOR THE ICE CREAM
240ml soya yoghurt
200–240ml plain soya milk
5 tbsp maple syrup or brown rice syrup
   (or a combination)
2 tsp vanilla

FOR THE RASPBERRY SORBET
200g sugar
300g raspberries
125ml sweet white wine

SERVES FOUR TO SIX

I really wanted to serve ice cream with sorbet as my dessert, as it's simple to make and always goes down a treat, but one of my guests was vegan and I wasn't sure how to get round that. A friend of mine came up with the idea of making soya ice cream. Then in the chaos of the day itself I forgot to buy the dairy ingredients, so we all ended up with this. I liked it so much that from now on this dessert will remain strictly vegan for me.

1 For the ice cream, whiz the ingredients in a blender or food processor. Pour into an ice-cream machine and churn. Freeze in a suitable container until required.

2 For the sorbet, put the sugar into a saucepan with 300ml water, bring to the boil then simmer for 5 minutes. Remove from the heat and allow to cool. Whiz the raspberries in a blender or food processor, then add the cooled syrup and the sweet white wine. Pour into a suitable container and freeze for at least 2 hours.

3 Remove both ice cream and sorbet from the freezer 10 to 20 minutes before serving.

Juliet Harbutt
baked alaska

3 egg whites
180g caster sugar
2 small panettone
500ml tub vanilla ice cream
  (you won't need it all)

This is my mother's recipe. My mother was a wonderful, passionate cook and preparing food was her way of expressing her love. Baked Alaska was my absolute favourite and she would always cook it for me as a treat, a reward or for a special occasion.

1 Preheat the oven to 230°C/Gas 8.

2 Whisk the egg whites until very stiff and dry. Add the sugar 2 tbsp at a time and beat until dissolved. The resulting mixture should be stiff and shiny.

3 Cut each panettone horizontally into 2–3 circles and place on a baking tray lined with non-stick parchment paper. Put a scoop of vanilla ice cream in the centre of each circle of panettone, leaving a small gap all around. Dollop the meringue over each one, making sure it covers the ice cream and panettone completely right down to the paper-lined tray – don't leave any gaps or the ice cream will melt.

4 Put in the top of the oven for 4–5 minutes – no longer! – until delicately coloured. Serve immediately.

Ian Cook

vodka-infused summer fruit jelly

5 punnets soft fruit, such as blackberries,
   raspberries, strawberries, blueberries
   and redcurrants
5–10 capfuls vodka
2 sachets vegan-approved powdered
   setting agent
225g caster sugar
fresh or soya pouring cream and icing
   sugar, to serve

SERVES FIVE

I wanted to serve something I could make well in
advance, something that was really light and easy on the
eye. I was careful to use vegan 'gelatine', so the dessert
was suitable for everyone. I ended up scoring 39/40! One
of the things this experience made me appreciate was
the benefit of meticulous planning. I planned the whole
day like a military operation and it paid off.

1 Divide the ripe fruit between 5 small glasses. Keep
some berries back for decoration. Drizzle the vodka (to
taste) over the fruit, put the glasses on a tray and chill
in the fridge.

2 Put the vegan setting agent in 425ml hot (not boiling)
water. Add the sugar, stir until dissolved, then let it sit at
room temperature for 1–2 minutes.

3 Remove the chilled fruit from the fridge. Divide the jelly
mixture between the glasses. Some of the fruit might rise
to the top, so push it back down. With all the fruit well
sealed by jelly, put the glasses in a bowl of ice and return
to the fridge to set for at least 1 hour.

4 To serve, dip each glass into hot water to loosen the jelly,
then turn it out onto a plate. Decorate the plates with the
reserved berries, dusted with icing sugar. Serve cold fresh
or soya cream alongside.

Linda Barker

lemon surprise pudding

70g unsalted butter, at room temperature
180g caster sugar
2 tsp grated lemon zest
3 medium eggs, separated
60g plain flour, sifted
250ml milk
100ml lemon juice
icing sugar, for dusting
fresh cream and raspberries, to serve

A dish that looks impressive but is really simple to make. This rises to a soufflé on top and leaves a lovely lemony sauce on the bottom – it's got the wow factor, and is really light to the taste. I practised a number of possible desserts on friends and family, and this one won by a distance – everyone loved it.

1 Preheat the oven to 200°C/Gas 6.

2 Beat the butter, sugar and lemon zest together until pale. Beat in the egg yolks, one at a time. Beat in the flour and milk alternately, little by little, until you have a smooth batter. Add the lemon juice.

3 Whip the egg whites until firm, then fold in.

4 Pour the mixture into 4 × 250ml ramekins. Bake in a bain-marie (in a baking tray half-filled with boiling water) for 20–25 minutes until slightly browned. Serve immediately with a sprinkling of icing sugar and, if you like, some fresh cream and raspberries.

Mica Paris

lemon vodka sorbet

lemon sorbet (shop-bought)
Polish vodka

I absolutely love vodka – it's one of my favourite drinks, because it's so clean on the palate. This was the perfect dessert for my dinner party, as it followed my Jamaican curried chicken, a very rich dish. This is zesty and lemony, and leaves guests tingly, refreshed and – let's be honest – a little bit tipsy.

1 Place 2 scoops of lemon sorbet into a chilled glass and add vodka to taste.

Edward Davies

mocha gateau

30–36 petit beurre biscuits
3 tbsp Camp coffee
1 tbsp Kahlúa (optional)
flaked almonds and grated chocolate, to
    decorate (or decoration of your choice)

FOR THE ICING
100g butter
8 tbsp icing sugar, sieved
1 egg, separated

This is full of childhood memories for me as it was my mother's signature dessert. She used to come back from holidays in France laden down with petit beurre biscuits because you couldn't get them in British shops. The key to success is to judge the amount of soaking time correctly – too little and the biscuits won't soften up enough, too much and they may start to disintegrate. Keep a careful eye on them and you'll be fine.

1 Mix together the Camp coffee and Kahlúa (if using) with 1 tbsp water.

2 For the icing, cream the butter by beating it with a wooden spoon, then add the icing sugar and egg yolk. Add a little of the coffee mixture to give flavour and colour. Whisk the egg white into stiff peaks and fold into the icing.

3 Dip 6 biscuits, one at a time, in the coffee mixture for a few seconds, then arrange on a plate in an oblong. Cover with a layer of icing, then make another layer of biscuits, and continue building the cake up until it is 5 or 6 biscuits deep. Use the remaining icing to cover the cake all over. Leave to set. Decorate the cake just before serving.

James Paley

baileys bread & butter pudding

1 medium-sized brioche
butter at room temperature
50g raisins (soaked overnight
   in the Baileys, if you like)
100ml Baileys, or to taste
300ml full-fat milk
2 eggs and 1 egg yolk
100g sugar

SERVES FOUR TO SIX

Bread and butter pudding is a proper English classic that my granny used to cook, but it has a tendency to be a bit bland and stodgy. So I wondered what it would be like with brioche, a deliciously light French bread. You can judge the results for yourself. It's good with any liqueur – I've often used Cointreau – but for me Baileys works best of all.

1 Trim the brioche of its crust (unless the crust is nice and soft) and cut into slices about 1–2cm thick. Lightly butter on both sides. Arrange the brioche in overlapping layers in an ovenproof dish, scattering the raisins as you go. Pour the Baileys over the brioche.

2 Beat together the milk, eggs, egg yolk and half the sugar. Pour slowly and evenly over the brioche, then set aside for at least 30 minutes for the liquid to be soaked up.

3 Preheat the oven to 180°C/Gas 4. Just before cooking, sprinkle the remaining sugar over the pudding. Bake for 30 minutes, until the top is golden and crusty. Serve warm.

Stuart Burke

raspberry & peaches with glazed meringue

5 peaches
75g sugar
1 vanilla pod, halved lengthways
    and seeds scraped out
250g raspberries
2 egg whites

SERVES FIVE

We filmed in the summer, and this is a perfect recipe for that time of year as it's so refreshing. But it could work equally well in winter, too, with apple and currants, maybe a bit of cinnamon and nutmeg. It's easy and quick, so you get something that looks very fancy for not too much effort. If I can do it, any old idiot can do it!

1 Preheat the oven to 180°C/Gas 4.

2 Peel and roughly chop the peaches. Cook gently with 1 tbsp water, a little of the sugar (about a tablespoon) and the vanilla seeds until the peaches are slightly softened and juicy. Add the raspberries, then divide the fruit between 5 ramekins.

3 Whisk the egg whites until stiff and dry. Gradually whisk in the remaining sugar, a little at a time, beating well until the mixture is glossy. Using a piping bag or a spoon, cover the ramekins with meringue. Bake for 10 minutes until golden brown.

Natalie Clarke

banoffee pie

397g tin condensed milk
15 digestives (half a pack)
125g unsalted or lightly salted butter
5 bananas
250ml fresh whipping or double cream

This is my mother-in-law's recipe, what I call a good old 'back to basics' pudding. I usually make it ahead of time then keep it in the fridge. If you do the same, be sure to take it out well before serving. Serve it straight from the fridge and your guests are likely to break their teeth on the biscuit base! It's very sweet but in a nice way – just don't overdo the portions.

1 Put the unopened tin of condensed milk in a saucepan, fill with water, cover with a lid then bring to the boil. Turn the heat down a little and leave to boil for 2 hours. Keep the lid on so the water doesn't all boil away; check on the pan from time to time. After 2 hours, take out the tin – carefully because it will be hot – and set it aside to cool down.

2 Crush the digestive biscuits in a bowl using something like the end of a rolling pin. (Or put them in a strong paper bag and run the rolling pin over them.) Melt the butter and pour over the biscuit crumbs. Mix together well then pour into a small springform cake tin (about 18cm) and press evenly over the base. Set aside to cool and firm up.

3 Slice the bananas and arrange over the cooled base. Open the tin of cooled condensed milk, now turned into a toffee-like sauce, and pour over the top. Set aside to cool. You can make it ahead up to this point.

4 Just before serving, whip the cream and put a thick layer on top of the banoffee pie.

John Santamaria

tiramisu

10 eggs, separated
240g granulated sugar
1kg mascarpone
finely grated zest of 2 lemons and 1 orange
strong espresso coffee, cold
Amaretto
400g Savoiardi biscuits (or sponge fingers)
4 tbsp cocoa powder

SERVES EIGHT TO TEN

Tiramisu – or 'Pick me up' as Italian waiters are fond of translating it to pretty customers – is my favourite dessert by far. My grandmother used to make it and then my father adapted the recipe by adding more Amaretto. Time permitting, I always make tiramisu for guests, as it appeals to both males (alcohol) and females (chocolate) and is visually pleasing.

1 Beat the egg yolks with the sugar until fluffy and pale, then stir in the mascarpone and the zests.

2 Beat the egg whites until they form stiff peaks like snow – you should be able to turn the bowl upside down over your head and not get wet! Slowly incorporate the mascarpone mixture into the egg whites.

3 Fill a deep bowl with espresso coffee and add a generous helping of Amaretto. Put the dish you want to make the tiramisu in on the side. Dip the sponge fingers one at a time in the coffee mixture – don't allow the biscuits to get so sodden they collapse – then use to cover the base of the tiramisu dish. When you have filled the dish with an even layer of sponge fingers, cover with a layer of mascarpone mixture, then sprinkle with cocoa powder. Repeat until you run out of ingredients and/or room! Refrigerate for at least 5 hours before serving.

Maria Greenhough

hot chocolate fondant with a lemon pot & raspberry coulis

FOR THE LEMON POT
100g caster sugar
juice and finely grated zest of 2 lemons
450ml double cream

FOR THE RASPBERRY COULIS
300g fresh or frozen raspberries
juice of 1 lemon
1–2 tbsp icing sugar (more if you
  prefer it sweeter)

FOR THE CHOCOLATE PUDDING
100g unsalted butter
100g good quality dark chocolate
2 large eggs
100g caster sugar
20g plain flour

SERVES FOUR

You get two for the price of one here! The richness of the chocolate is complemented by the tartness of the lemon pots. With the chocolate recipe coming all the way from Australia and the lemon pots from Yorkshire, this dessert is truly a worldwide offering.

1 For the lemon pots, put the sugar, lemon zest and double cream in a heavy-based pan and bring to the boil, stirring occasionally until the sugar is dissolved, then boil for 3 minutes. Take off the heat and stir in most of the lemon juice. Taste for lemon zing, then add more juice if desired. If you don't want the lemon zest in the finished dish, strain the lemon cream at this point. Pour into 4 ramekins or small dishes (125–150ml capacity). Allow to cool, then cover and chill in the fridge for a few hours until set.

2 For the raspberry coulis, place the raspberries in a saucepan, add the lemon juice and mash with a fork, then sift in the icing sugar, stir well and place over a low heat. When the raspberries are just simmering, take off the heat and pour through a sieve into a jug, pushing the juice through with a wooden spoon. Chill for a few hours.

3 Melt the butter and chocolate in a dish over a pan of simmering water. Once melted, set aside to cool. Meanwhile, whisk the eggs, caster sugar and flour together by hand until smooth. Stir in the cooled chocolate mixture until smooth and blended. Pour into 4 buttered ramekins and set aside.

4 When almost ready to serve, preheat the oven to 200°C /Gas 6. Cook the chocolate fondants for 12–15 minutes until set. Serve hot, inverted onto dessert plates, with the lemon pots placed alongside and the jug of raspberry coulis passed around the table.

Top Ten
Winners' Menus

Ian Cook

AVERAGE SCORE OF 9.3

A customer services manager from Liverpool, Ian, thirty-nine, has come the nearest of any *Come Dine With Me* contestant to achieving full marks: all but one of his guests awarded him a ten, with the other only giving one mark less because he served water in plastic bottles and bread on a chipped plate. Like all the other contestants in his week, he knew he was catering for a vegan, and designed his menu so that most of the dishes were the same for all his guests, to make his vegan diner feel included, though he did also serve a non-vegan main course of roasted wild seabass. Meticulous planning was also a key feature of his approach – and although he still had quite a lot to do at the last minute, he made sure he'd done lots of preparation early in the day.

STARTER
Roasted butternut squash and red lentil soup with pesto oil and garlic croutons (page 90).

VEGAN MAIN COURSE
Fillet of tofu and chestnut with garlic potato cakes and spicy tomato sauce (page 100).

DESSERT
Vodka-infused summer fruit jelly (page 160).

Benito Gundin

AVERAGE SCORE OF 8.3

Spanish-born Benito scored 25 out of 30 with his menu
that kicked off with the classic Jewish starter of latkes,
a form of potato cake. As a non-meat-eater, he opted for
fish for his main, then finished off his menu with a classic
tart, all washed down with matching wines for each
course. As a side dish to his main course, he made a
ratatouille with red and yellow peppers, to represent
the colours in the Spanish flag.

STARTER
Latkes and grilled vegetables with goat's
cheese and basil oil
(page 64).

MAIN COURSE
Baked seabass with potatoes, fennel and
tomato sauce
(page 106).

DESSERT
Almond and pear tart
(page 148).

Jim Blythe

AVERAGE SCORE OF 8.5

A university lecturer from Cardiff, Jim's menu consisted of recipes he'd picked up during his travels – such as his Brazilian main course, which was accompanied by a root vegetable, manioc, that needs careful handling because it's poisonous when raw. Even though his guests could barely read the main course, which he presented in Portuguese, the different combinations of flavours hit the spot.

STARTER
Pork satay with courgette salad
(page 89).

MAIN COURSE
Chicken in Bahian sauce with manioc
(page 115).

DESSERT
Glazed pears with coffee cream
(page 143).

Linda Barker

Interior design guru and broadcaster Linda was cooking for three fellow celebrities – Lee Ryan, Peter Stringfellow and Michelle Heaton. Her choice of starter meant she only had to reheat the food just before serving, and the potatoes dauphinoise, which she served alongside her main, could be prepared in advance. The lemon surprise pudding was a tricky feat to pull off as she could only prepare it just before serving – but she pulled it off, to share the charity prize with Lee.

STARTER
Cauliflower soup with goat's cheese and truffle oil and home-made rolls (page 95).

MAIN COURSE
Herb-crusted lamb with mint sauce
(page 118).

DESSERT
Lemon surprise pudding (page 162) and 'dog' biscuits (page 173) served with cheese

Mica Paris

Singer and TV presenter Mica went back to her Jamaican roots for her menu, including the classic dish of ackee – a fruit that's related to pineapple – with saltfish. The food certainly hit the spot as she averaged 9 out of 10 from her celebrity diners: Ulrika Jonsson, Ben de Lisi, Dave Quantick and Helen Lederer.

STARTER
Ackee and salt cod served with plantains and pineapple (page 62).

MAIN COURSE
Jamaican chicken with rice and peas (pages 116–17).

DESSERT
Lemon vodka sorbet (page 163).

James Paley

AVERAGE SCORE OF 7.3

Pub manager James was first to cook in Coventry and decided to offer a choice for each course. (We've given a selection of his dishes in this menu.) That left him with a lot of work to do, and things became even more hectic when his grill wouldn't quite work as he wanted, while a mixing bowl smashed during his pudding prep. Luckily, living above the pub he runs, he was able to find replacement crockery, and kept his cool to walk off with the prize.

STARTER
Crab and red pepper soup (page 96) *and* black pudding and apple tower (page 63).

MAIN COURSE
Fillet steak with mushroom, pancetta and port sauce and parsnip crisps (page 129).

DESSERT
Baileys bread and butter pudding (page 165).

Juliet Harbutt

Food writer Juliet is a lover of cheese, and in 1994 created the British Cheese Awards. Before serving her pudding, she presented a board of local cheeses, including Little Wallop, a small goat's cheese wrapped in a vine leaf, made by the Evenlode Partnership (which is Juliet herself and Alex James, ex-bass guitarist of Blur). The pudding was her trickiest course. Baked Alaska needs to be timed exactly to make sure the ice cream doesn't melt inside the meringue. But she pulled off this tricky feat, earning a score of 24 out of 30, even though one of her guests was not a fan of cheese.

STARTER
Arbroath smokies pâté with roasted red peppers and red onions (page 80).

MAIN COURSE
Teriyaki roast salmon steaks
(page 102).

DESSERT
Baked Alaska
(page 159).

Jane Bates

Jane admits to being something of a celebrity stalker – whenever she sees a famous face, she'll insist on getting a photo with them. So she decided to give her dinner a Hollywood theme – naming all her dishes after film stars, and asking her guests to dress up as their favourite celebrity (as well as laying on a red carpet and fake paparazzi to pretend to take the diners' photos). It all seemed to hit the spot as Jane ran out the winner of the competition in Manchester.

STARTER
Lock, stock and smokin' salmon, aka Vinny Jones
(page 67).

MAIN COURSE
Pirates' planked steak, aka Johnny Depp
(page 127).

DESSERT
Little ol' wine jelly, aka Dean Martin
(page 150).

Daniel Fletcher

AVERAGE SCORE OF 8.3

Part-French web designer Daniel was the youngest contestant during the competition in Derby, and his guests didn't expect much from him. He took the risk of writing his menu in French, which meant that none of his diners knew what they'd be served until it arrived at the table. But his classic Gallic menu – balancing a cold starter with a hot main and a chilled, pre-prepared dessert, hit the spot, making him a worthy winner.

STARTER
Terrine of spring onion and chicken in Parma ham
(page 74).

MAIN COURSE
Duck à la pêche et à l'orange
(page 133).

DESSERT
French summer fruit pudding with mascarpone
(page 157).

Ronnie Masters

AVERAGE SCORE OF 7.3

Ronnie, PR for a successful catering firm in Bristol, took some tips from her own chef to ensure she came out on top with her menu. She also made sure the guests got exactly what they wanted by cooking her steaks to order – even redoing one of them when it wasn't quite right. She also washed everything down with copious amounts of wine – so much so that one of her guests fell asleep during dessert. But it all seemed to work, as Ronnie walked off with the £1,000 prize at the end of the week.

STARTER
Asparagus salad with lemon and shallot dressing
(page 77).

MAIN COURSE
Tournedos on celeriac and potato rosti with a wild mushroom stroganoff (page 139).

DESSERT
Warm banana tarts served with ice cream and rum
(page 151).

index

acknowledgements

The publishers would like to thank all the following volunteer recipe testers: Polly Andrews, Jennifer Austin, Alison Barrow, Emma Buckley, Carli Burgos, Christelle Chamouton, Lynsey Dalladay, Samantha Eades, Dave Emsley, Sarah Emsley, Val Emsley, Linda Evans, Lisa Gordon, Sharon Gordon, Sophie Holmes, Kate Jennings, Samantha Jones, Julie Lam, Toni Lance, Sheila Lee, Alison Martin, Fiona Murphy, Charlotte Nash, Barry O'Donovan, Nuala O'Neill, Tom Poland, Gareth Pottle, Elizabeth Rizzo, Nick Robinson, Richard Shailer, Marianne Velmans, Susanna Wadeson, Rachel Walters, Alma Weber, Sarah Whittaker, Sophie Wilson, Eleanor Wood, Doug Young.

Every effort has been made to obtain the necessary permissions with reference to illustrative copyright material. We apologize for any omissions in this respect and will be pleased to make the appropriate acknowledgements in any future edition. All contestant pictures are courtesy of Granada and the *Come Dine With Me* winners with the exception of Linda Barker and Peter Stringfellow © James Bandey; Linda Lusardi © Mark Johnson.